DOING THE PUBLIC GOOD

DOING THE

PUBLIC GOOD

Latina/o Scholars Engage Civic Participation

Edited by

Kenneth P. González and

Raymond V. Padilla

STERLING, VIRGINIA

COPYRIGHT © 2008

BY STYLUS PUBLISHING, LLC.

The following poems by Jennifer Ayala

Copyright © 2008 by Jennifer Ayala
"If you ask me who I am"
"My childhood smells like fresh rain on the pavement"
"Am I like fading footprints in the snow?"
"I am a witness/perpetrator of violence"
"The game of standards"
"With sisters, brothers, allies, I am/we are actors"

"I Am Joaquin" copyright © 1969 By Rodolfo "Corky" Gonzales

Published by Stylus Publishing, LLC
22883 Quicksilver Drive
Sterling, Virginia 20166-2102

Library of Congress Cataloging-in-Publication-Data
Doing the public good : Latina/o scholars engage civic participation / edited by Kenneth P. González and Raymond V. Padilla.
p. cm.
Includes index.
ISBN 978-1-57922-262-8 (hardcover : alk. paper)—ISBN 978-1-57922-263-5 (pbk. : alk. paper) 1. Education, Higher—Aims and objectives—United States. 2. Civics—Study and teaching—United States. 3. Political participation—United States. 4. Hispanic American college teachers. I. González, Kenneth P., 1968– II. Padilla, Raymond V.
LA227.4.D65 2008
378'.015—dc22

ISBN: 978-1-57922-262-8 (cloth)
ISBN: 978-1-57922-263-5 (paper)

Printed in the United States of America

All first editions printed on acid free paper
that meets the American National Standards Institute
Z39-48 Standard.

Bulk Purchases

Quantity discounts are available for use in workshops
and for staff development.
Call 1-800-232-0223

First Edition, 2008

10 9 8 7 6 5 4 3 2 1

Our thanks to Rodolfo "Corky" Gonzales for permission to reprint "I Am Joaquin," which became the anthem for the Chicano Civil Rights Movement of the 1960s.

Our thanks to Ray García for permission to use his artwork for the book cover.

To my father and mother, who inspired me to serve the public good. To my son and daughter, Kaél Joaquín and Xiomara-Mia, may the stories of these good men and women guide you to a vocation of love and hope. To my wife, Elizabeth Gil-González, thank you for being my partner in the service of the public good.

—KENNETH P. GONZÁLEZ

To all those who have done the public good.

—RAYMOND V. PADILLA

CONTENTS

1. LATINA/O FACULTY PERSPECTIVES ON HIGHER
   EDUCATION FOR THE PUBLIC GOOD   *1*
   An Intergenerational Approach
   Kenneth P. González and Raymond V. Padilla

2. *RES PUBLICA*   *13*
   Chicano Evolving Poetics of the Public Good
   Raymond V. Padilla

3. *VOCES* IN DIALOGUE   *25*
   What Is Our Work in the Academy?
   Jennifer Ayala

4. *TRES HERMANAS* (THREE SISTERS)   *39*
   A Model of Relational Achievement
   Aída Hurtado, María A. Hurtado, and Arcelia L. Hurtado

5. TWO BROTHERS IN HIGHER EDUCATION   *61*
   Weaving a Social Fabric for Service in Academia
   Miguel Guajardo and Francisco Guajardo

6. AGENCY AND THE GAME OF CHANGE   *83*
   Contradictions, *Consciencia*, and Self-Reflection
   Luis Urrieta Jr.

7. TOWARD PUBLIC EDUCATION AS A PUBLIC GOOD   *97*
   Reflections from the Field
   Caroline Sotello Viernes Turner

8. FOR THE PUBLIC GOOD   *113*
   A Personal Reflection
   Flora V. Rodriguez-Brown

9. IN SEARCH OF PRAXIS   *125*
    Legacy Making in the Aggregate
    Kenneth P. González

10. *LA TRENZA DE IDENTIDADES*   *135*
    Weaving Together My Personal, Professional,
    and Communal Identities
    Dolores Delgado Bernal

11. LATINA/O *CUENTOS* SHAPE A NEW MODEL OF HIGHER
    EDUCATION FOR THE PUBLIC GOOD   *149*
    Kenneth P. González and Raymond V. Padilla

    CONTRIBUTORS   *155*

    INDEX   *161*

KENNETH P. GONZÁLEZ

RAYMOND V. PADILLA

I

LATINA/O FACULTY PERSPECTIVES ON HIGHER EDUCATION FOR THE PUBLIC GOOD

An Intergenerational Approach

Kenneth P. González and Raymond V. Padilla

S ince their inception, American universities have existed, in large part, to prepare students for active citizenship and to produce knowledge that serves the needs of society (Bringle, 1999). Today, however, many leaders in higher education warn that American universities are losing a central piece of their historic identity and purpose (Bok, 2003; Boyer, 1994; Checkoway, 2001; Newmann, 2000). These scholars claim that most colleges and universities have, in fact, drifted away from their civic missions. They argue, for example, that faculty members are more aligned with the narrow expectations of their departments and professional associations than with the needs of society. They insist that faculty are neither adequately trained nor prepared for civic roles and responsibilities, and they highlight the lack of faculty rewards and incentives to engage directly with local communities.

Evidence also exists that students are less interested in civic participation than previous generations were (Bennett, 1997; Hart, 1997; Mortenson, 2006; Putnam, 1996). Researchers note declining numbers of voters, decreased interest in volunteer activities, and large-scale apathy toward the election process. Bennett (1997), moreover, found that student interest in civic engagement actually declines during the college years. Critics of higher education point to a curriculum that is increasingly disconnected from societal life outside the walls of college campuses.

In addition, some critics argue that administrators' fixation with fundraising has clouded their sense of academic purpose and civic values. Derek Bok (2003), for example, describes the growing development of commercialization on college campuses. He defines commercialization as efforts to sell the work of universities for profit, and he describes how patent licensing programs, for-profit ventures in Internet education, and athletics have led universities to become increasingly commercialized. Commercialization, Bok argues, threatens higher education's civic mission by shifting the focus away from the legitimate needs of students and society to revenue and market forces.

Concomitantly, it is important to note that a number of institutions and national organizations have increased efforts to rebuild a sense of civic participation among students and faculty. Campus Compact, for example, is a national organization of more than 900 colleges and universities committed to the civic mission of higher education. The organization supports efforts to increase (a) student participation in community service activities, (b) partnerships between campuses and local communities, and (c) integration of community engagement into faculty research and teaching (Campus Compact, 2003). More recently, the University of Michigan, along with nine other universities, launched the "Diverse Democracy Project" whose primary goal is to explore how colleges and universities are creating diverse learning environments and actively preparing students to live and work in a diverse democracy (Hurtado, Engberg, Ponjuan, & Landreman, 2002).

Despite the efforts noted above, many argue that such projects remain at the margins of university priorities and activities (Boyte, 1998; Checkoway, 2001; Newmann, 2000). Boyte (1998) insists that "for the concept of civic renewal to really take hold, a substantial cultural change is needed" (p. 2). Other scholars and leaders in higher education agree and call for nothing short of a social movement to restore higher education's civic mission. In 1995, the W. K. Kellogg Foundation initiated the support of such a movement. Early on, the Kellogg Foundation targeted specific institutional projects that addressed the civic mission of higher education. Results of those projects led to the creation of the Kellogg Forum on Higher Education for the Public Good (The Forum) (Kellogg Foundation for Higher Education, 2004). With a singular focus on advancing the public service role of American higher education, The Forum builds alliances, develops strategies, and plans activities that contribute to a new, broader agenda.

Recognizing faculty members as a key constituency to support the civic mission of higher education, a primary activity of The Forum includes convening "Intergenerational Scholars Symposiums." Designed to foster relationships between senior and "emerging" scholars, participants in the symposiums attempt to (a) define the concept of scholarship related to the public good, (b) formulate research agendas that connect scholarship to broader societal needs, and (c) identify avenues for disseminating "public good" research. Although some progress has been made (Hurtado, 2007; Kezar, Chambers, & Burkhart, 2005; Martinez, Pasque, Bowman, & Chambers, 2005), it is clear that a great deal more reflection and discussion are needed to sufficiently address these important tasks.

Inspired by the work of The Forum, this book attempts to engage an intergenerational group of Latina/o scholars in personal and critical reflection about how their work as faculty members connects with the civic mission of the university. The underlying rationale for such a project was that any effort toward lasting change must begin with reflection. The decision to focus on Latina/o faculty members was based on the following arguments: (a) the commitment of Latina/o academics in the United States to the principles of higher education for the public good can be traced back to the Civil Rights Movement and the development of *El Plan de Santa Barbara* (Chicano Coordinating Council on Higher Education, 1970), and (b) Latino/a faculty, more often than not, continue to engage themselves in activities that directly serve local communities (Antonio, 2002).

The Historic Commitment of Latina/o Faculty to Higher Education for the Public Good

The Latino population of the United States resulted from the confluence of diverse peoples, histories, languages, and cultures. In this population, the very concept of higher education and its connection to community and the public good is filtered through various cultural perspectives that shift over time, so that it is not easy to describe any single view of the notion. Nevertheless, some general characterization still is possible if one looks at the distinct historical influences and how they may have shaped the contemporary views of Latina/os on higher education and the public good. For many Latina/os, the chief influences on higher education and the public good derive from the historic developments in higher education as experienced by the Spanish, on the one hand, and by various Native American cultures on the other, especially the Aztecs. A mixture of these influences is an important factor that shaped the perspectives of U.S. Latina/os once they found themselves in significant numbers in American institutions of higher education during the middle of the 20th century.

During the Middle Ages, Spain was a center of higher learning in Europe. Located at the crossroads between Europe and Africa, Spain became an important nexus between the higher learning of the Moorish conquerors who settled on the Iberian peninsula and the rest of medieval Europe. In 1254, during the rein of Alfonso X, *el Sabio* (the wise king), the University of Salamanca received a charter, thus becoming one of the earliest centers of higher learning in all of Europe. In solidifying the university, the king was clearly mindful of the beneficial effects that higher learning can bestow on society. The University of Salamanca became a model for universities in the Americas during the colonial period.

Hundreds of miles across the Atlantic ocean, a number of Native American cultures had reached such high levels of development that they also created institutions of higher learning. The Aztecs in particular developed the *calmecac* as an important such institution. Aztec learning in general was guided by the concept of cultivating *rostro y corazon* (the head—literally, the face—and the heart). This philosophy of education clearly emphasized the public aspects of education and the community-centered nature of Aztec society. The Aztec philosophy of education also emphasized both the integral and the instrumental aspects of education, since it emphasized the development of both rhetorical and military skills. The Aztec ideal of the cultivated individual resonates with the widespread view of education in Hispanic culture that sees a well-educated person as one who is *bien educado*, meaning that the person has abiding values, civil comportment, and decency, in addition to technical competence. Technical competence alone or mere schooling does not create a person who is *bien educado*. Therefore, there is a distinction between someone who is merely well schooled and someone who is *bien educado*. In this perspective, higher education fits into a social schema where highly educated people play positive roles in their community, thus earning the respect and admiration of the community. It also expects that a person who has received an advanced education will display the characteristics of someone who is *bien educado*. Failure to do so implies a loss of community respect and admiration. So in Hispanic culture, the tradition is for institutions of higher education and the people who pass through them to enhance the public good through their technical competence and their presumed superior moral development and character.

With the Europeans' conquest of the Americas, a mestizo culture developed during the colonial period that displayed the influences of Spain (and the rest of Europe) as well as the native cultures. When Spain conquered the native peoples, the country was still under the influence of medieval traditions, with the church continuing to play a significant role in the affairs of state. The medieval church, in turn, had been the center of higher learning in Europe for centuries, so higher learning as practiced by the church was influential in the development of higher education in the Americas. However, this influence was filtered through the conquest and its aftermath. Most notably, the early development of higher education in the Americas was in line with the needs of a proselytizing church that saw its magisterial role with respect to native populations as both spiritual and practical. These two tendencies are evident in the contrasting missions of a college such as Colegio San Nicolas Hidalgo, founded in 1540 to pursue theology and religion, and the educational programs of Vasco de Quiroga during the same period around Lake Patzcuaro, where arts and crafts for the native populations were the main focus. From the higher education traditions developed in Mexico during the colonial period, two ideas continued to influence the thinking of later generations of Latina/os. First, there is a definite utopian influence in the teachings of Vasco de Quiroga. Second, there is a deep concern for the well-being and progress of the community. Following the independence of Mexico, higher education institutions in that country began to develop a significant political role, more so than is customary for postsecondary institutions in the United States. This political role of Latin American higher education is evident in the long history of the Royal and Pontifical University of Mexico, which was founded in 1551 and later became the Autonomous National University of Mexico (UNAM). Thus, by the time of the Chicano Movement in the late 1960s, all of these historic influences helped to shape Hispanic ideals about the role and function of colleges and universities in the United States, particularly with respect to their role in promoting the well-being of the Hispanic community.

The United States' conquest of northern Mexico in the middle of the

19th century brought to the fore a whole new set of influences on Hispanics and higher education in the United States. Following the conquest, and responding to the needs of an agrarian but rapidly expanding industrial society, U.S. policy on higher education shifted significantly with the enactment in the second half of the 19th century of federal legislation designed to promote the development of science, industry, and agriculture. The "land grant universities" were committed to improving society through the application of science and advanced learning. Unfortunately, the conditions of the U.S. Hispanic population at the time did not promote their participation in the newly founded institutions. The postconquest years were filled with tension and dislocation for the U.S. Hispanic population that entailed struggles related to land ownership, citizenship, and racial discrimination. It was not until the early 20th century, during the period of the Mexican Revolution, that the U.S. Hispanic population began to stabilize and eventually increase significantly in size. However, many of the new immigrants throughout the 20th century were not prepared to enter U.S. institutions of higher learning. In fact, they had considerable difficulty just completing high school. By the 1960s, the educational conditions of U.S. Hispanics had become so dire that major efforts were launched to improve the educational success of this population.

It was in this context of educational neglect that the Chicano Movement, along with other Hispanic movements, developed in the United States during the 1960s. However, there had already been a long tradition of activism in this community as exemplified by the work of the League for United Latin American Citizens (LULAC), the American G.I. Forum, and numerous other organizations that developed throughout the 20th century. The uniqueness of the movements of the 1960s was their militancy and demands for radical social change. In addition, they were led mostly by young people, often high school and college students. Out of this social ferment, *El plan espiritual de Aztlan* and *El plan de Santa Barbara* were crafted as foundational positions to guide the spiritual, ethical, educational, and material development of the Hispanic community. The focus of *El plan de Santa Barbara* was educational, within an ideology of liberation. In this plan, there was a clear understanding of the important role that postsecondary institutions play in community development. They were seen as the engines of progress for the Hispanic community. However, the performance of these institutions was seen as wanting and out of sync with the historic need to transform

Hispanic communities so they could become viable once again. As a result, the plan called for students to become the vanguard of social mobilization. In particular, students were to organize themselves into one national organization that would be called *El Movimiento Estudiantil Chicano de Aztlan* (MEChA), and to establish Chicano studies programs in colleges and universities. The students' main role would be to increase the college attendance of Hispanic students and to help solve problems that plagued their communities. Thus, from its very beginning, Chicano and Hispanic activism has emphasized the importance of higher education and its responsibility to promote the public good.

The students' activism expanded during the 1970s and '80s to include young professionals as well. As a result, professionals became active in Hispanic caucuses or special interest groups that were created in national organizations such as the American Educational Research Association (AERA), the American Association for Higher Education (AAHE), and many others. At the same time, this generation of Hispanics established many new organizations that sought to improve educational outcomes for U.S. Hispanics. These included state organizations such as the Association of Chicanos for College Admissions (ACCA), the Texas Association of Chicanos in Higher Education (TACHE), the Raza Association of Chicanos in Higher Education (RACHE), and a number of others. At the national level, traditional organizations such as LULAC and the G.I. Forum pursued similar goals, but new ones, such as the Coordinating Council on Higher Education, the Hispanic Scholarship Fund, and, more recently, the American Association of Hispanics in Higher Education (AAHHE), did as well. All of these Hispanic organizations, along with numerous others, continued the tradition of linking higher education to the public good.

One interesting parallel development during this same period was the establishment of alternative institutions of higher education for Hispanics, including Colegio Cesar Chavez, Colegio de la Tierra, Universidad de Campesinos Libres, Colegio Jacinto Treviño, Lincoln-Juarez University, and DQU. All of these institutions were committed to the development of Hispanic communities through higher education, and, although most of them did not last very long, the National Hispanic University exists today as heir to the great experiment in independent Hispanic higher education of the mid-20th century. So whether one examines the Spanish, indigenous, or modern influences on Hispanics and higher education, there is a consistent preoccupation with the use of higher education to pursue the public good.

Acquiring Latina/o Faculty Perspectives: Autoethnography

To acquire faculty perspectives on higher education for the public good, we asked a number of senior-, mid-, and early-career scholars to participate in an autoethnographic research project. We chose autoethnography (Ellis & Bochner, 2000) because of its ability to connect personal experiences with cultural contexts. Ellis and Bochner defined autoethnography as an "autobiographical genre of writing and research that displays multiple layers of consciousness, connecting the personal to the cultural" (p. 739). Usually written in first-person voice, autoethnographies are represented in such forms as short stories, poetry, personal essays, journals, and social science prose (Ellis & Bochner, 2000). As a means of producing autoethnographies, each of the participants wrote about the relationship between his or her work as a faculty member and serving the needs of society. To help guide faculty reflections, the following open-ended prompts were provided for senior-, mid-, and early-career scholars:

Senior Scholars: (a) In what ways has your work as a Latina/o faculty member responded to the civic mission of higher education? In what ways has it not? (b) What have been some of the obstacles, both personal and institutional, that have hampered your ability to address the civic mission of higher education? (c) What has facilitated your ability to address the civic mission of higher education? (d) What would you change, both personally and institutionally, to better serve society in your role as a faculty member?

Mid-/Early-Career Scholars: (a) In what ways do you see your work responding to the civic mission of higher education? In what ways does your work not respond to this mission? (b) In what ways has your doctoral training (or early faculty career experiences) prepared you to respond to the civic mission of higher education? In what ways has it not? (c) What vision do you have of serving the public in your role as a faculty member? The following section summarizes the primary themes of each autoethnography.

Latina/o Faculty Autoethnographies

In chapter 2, Raymond V. Padilla sets in motion this collection of faculty reflections by illuminating the relationship between the public and private good, reminding the reader that the public good is "almost always based on someone's frame of reference" (p. 17). Padilla then provides a series of conceptual anchors that help structure an understanding of the public good. For example, he borrows the concept of "organic knowledge" (González, 1995) to describe the process by which individuals come to perceive and know the public good. The chapter concludes with an approach to serving the public good rooted in notions of art.

In chapter 3, Jennifer Ayala uses poetry and prose to bring into focus the limits and promise of advancing the public good in the context of American higher education. She describes the mechanisms that reproduce chasms between universities and the communities they were designed to serve. She makes it clear that promoting the public good requires "bridge work," which refers to building or being the bridge between the university and the community. Ayala's chapter ends with an example of research and teaching that integrates academic work with community and what she calls "spirit work."

Chapter 4, written by *las tres hermanas* (the three sisters) Aída, María, and Arcelia Hurtado, provides an intimate glimpse into the process of choosing to serve the public good. The authors illustrate how relationships with parents, siblings, teachers, and role models influence, support, and reproduce a process of identity formation firmly integrated with the public good. The authors highlight the role of opportunity and privilege in attaining positions of influence and stress the importance of giving back and addressing the needs of local communities.

In chapter 5, Miguel and Francisco Guajardo offer another vivid example of how family histories and regional cultures shape individual disposition toward the public good. They also present a model of promoting the public good rooted in Mexican traditions that go back several generations: *pláticas*. The authors define *pláticas* as spaces for sharing stories, ideas, and experiences. They conclude with a vision of serving the public good that is based on the interdependence between universities and the communities that surround them.

Chapter 6, written by Luis Urrieta Jr., presents a series of tough questions for Latina/o faculty who purport to be engaged in and concerned about social justice issues. Urrieta argues that any effort to advance the public good must coexist with critical self-reflection about motives, purpose, strategy, and outcome. He offers a distinction between what it means to "play the game" versus "selling out." Finally, he highlights a process for recognizing individual agency in an institution marked by a history of White supremacy and patriarchy.

In chapter 7, Caroline Sotello Viernes Turner describes her personal path toward serving the public good. She reveals barriers and support systems that make up the context in which work toward the public good occurs. She ends her chapter with criteria one can use to assess the extent to which colleges and universities do, in fact, serve the public good.

Chapter 8, written by Flora Rodriguez-Brown, illustrates the historical context of Latina/o professors working toward the public good in American higher education. Using a series of concrete examples, Rodriguez-Brown reveals layers of organizational structure and individual acts contaminated with racist and sexist ideology. She then provides an example of sacrifice and success that comes with engaging the public good.

In chapter 9, Kenneth P. González brings to light the influence of parents, specifically his father, in developing a vision for the public good. He challenges existing notions of faculty work and questions the extent to which faculty have contributed to the public good. González concludes by offering alternative approaches and priorities for professors seeking tangible, social change.

Chapter 10, written by Dolores Delgado Bernal, draws attention to the power of stories or *cuentos* in shaping our personal and professional vocation. She uses the concepts of *trenza* and *mujerista* sensibilities to describe a holistic approach to faculty work that weaves together a woman's personal, professional, and communal identities. She asserts that weaving together one's multiple identities enhances both the quality of her work and the quality of her life.

The personal stories or *cuentos* that make up this volume open up necessary space for debate, imagination, and the possibility of professors in American higher education to better serve the public good. In the final chapter, Kenneth P. González and Raymond V. Padilla analyze the major insights that emerged from each *cuento*. The product of their analysis led to the shaping of a new model of higher education for the public good. The model, derived inductively, describes how we, as Latina/o professors (a) came to perceive and know the public good; (b) developed a sense of urgency to address it; (c) encountered various barriers in promoting it; and (d) used specific strategies to achieve it.

References

Antonio, A. (2002). Faculty of color reconsidered: Reassessing contributions to scholarship. *Journal of Higher Education, 73*, 582–602.

Bennett, S. E. (1997). Why young Americans hate politics and what we should do about it. *Political Science & Politics, 31*, 741–761.

Bok, D. (2003). *Universities in the marketplace.* Princeton, NJ: Princeton University Press.

Boyer, E. L. (1994, March 4). Creating the new American college. *Chronicle of Higher Education,* A48.

Boyte, H. (1998). The rebirth of citizenship. *Commonwealth, 125,* 14–16.

Bringle, R. (Ed.). (1999). *Colleges and universities as citizens.* Boston: Allyn & Bacon.

Campus Compact. (2003). *Service counts.* Providence, RI: Author.

Checkoway, B. (2001). Renewing the civic mission of the American research university. *Journal of Higher Education, 72,* 125–147.

Chicano Coordinating Council on Higher Education. (1970). *El plan de Santa Barbara: A Chicano plan for higher education.* Santa Barbara, CA: La Causa Publications.

Ellis, C., & Bochner, A. P. (2000). Autoethnography, personal narrative, reflexivity: Researcher as subject. In N. K. Denzin & Y. S. Lincoln (Eds.), *Handbook of qualitative research* (pp. 733–768). Thousand Oaks, CA: Sage.

González, M. C. (1995). In search of the voice I always had. In R. V. Padilla & R. C. Chávez (Eds)., *The leaning ivory tower* (pp. 77–90). Albany: State University of New York.

Hart, R. (1997). Children's participation: *The theory and practice of involving young citizens in community development and environmental care.* London: Earthscan.

Hurtado, S. (2007). Linking diversity with the educational and civic missions of higher education. *Review of Higher Education, 30,* 185–196.

Hurtado, S., Engberg, M. E., Ponjuan, L., & Landreman, L. (2002). Students' pre-college preparation for participation in a diverse democracy. *Research in Higher Education, 43,* 163–186.

Kellogg Forum on Higher Education for the Public Good. (2004). *Forum history.* Ann Arbor: MI: Author.

Kezar, A., Chambers, T., & Burkhardt, A. (Eds.). (2005). *Higher education for the public good: Emerging voices from a national movement.* San Francisco: Jossey-Bass.

Martinez, M., Pasque, P., Bowman, N., & Chambers, T. (2005). *Multidisciplinary perspectives on higher education for the public good.* Ann Arbor: University of Michigan.

Mortenson, T. (2006). *Where have all the students gone? Higher education by the numbers.* Oskaloosa, IA: Postsecondary Education Opportunity.

Newmann, F. (2000). *Saving higher education's soul.* Providence, RI: The Futures Project.

Padilla, R. V. (1993). Using dialogical research methods in group interviews. In D. L. Morgan (Ed.), *Successful focus group methods: Advancing the state of an art* (pp. 153–166). Newbury Park, CA: Sage.

Putnam, T. (1996). The strange disappearance of civic America. *The American Prospect, 24,* 33–44.

2

RES PUBLICA

Chicano Evolving Poetics of the Public Good

Raymond V. Padilla

There can be little question that in matters of the public good a key issue is to distinguish between the public and the private so that somehow the public good does not get swamped by private goodies. Yet, distinguishing between the public and the private can be a most vexing exercise. Veteran editors have discovered to their chagrin that only a slight orthographic slip, something as innocent as the omission of a modest "L" from the puritanical public, can expose the reader embarrassingly to the most intimate of private spaces. As an editor of many texts on public policy, I have learned to be especially respectful of the intricate, subtle, and delicate relationship between the public and the private. As a longtime activist in academia, I learned along the way to be mindful of the thin veil that separates the public from the private and how one can easily morph into the other.

Bread

We had just arrived from Mexico to our destination in the United States. My mother and all eight of her children, weary and hungry from the long trip, were huddled in the barn that stood by the side of the big house belonging to the new patron. It should have been nine children, but the eldest daughter, a mere teenager, had decided that she would not become a stranger in a foreign country and marry a Gringo. She stayed behind. I was fifth oldest of the now remaining eight children and hardly more than five years old. Recognizing that we must have been hungry, the patron*'s wife sent from the big house a loaf of bread and a jar of fruit preserves for us to eat. This surely had to be an act of generosity, an enhancement of the public good.*

But why was my mother so obviously angry? She who never minced words or held back her sentiments exploded with indignation and rage. The loaf of bread was covered with mold. "We are not animals!" she thundered. "Does she think that we are going to eat this filth?" My mother threw away the food offering and made sure that we had something wholesome to eat. To this day I have no idea what we finally ate, but it wasn't the moldy bread.

An experience like this can teach a young child many things about the world, including something about justice and the public good. This type of learning is very special, premised on what we might call "organic knowing," a term used by Cristina González (1995), who relates a similar learning experience but on an entirely different topic. Knowledge acquired organically seeps into the very pores of our being, not just into our consciousness. It is not just a lesson to remember, it is a lesson to live by. This kind of knowing shapes how we think but also who we are, how we live, and what we do with our lives. It is at the organic level of knowing that we learn to distinguish between the public and the private good. When this organic type of knowing is absent, the public and the private good can easily become entangled, a mere slip from one to the other.

Don Medina

In the 1950s we lived in Montopolis, easily the most destitute barrio *of Austin, the capital of the state of Texas. With the help of the* patron*'s wife, now a widow, my father bought two small lots in what once had been a vacant field at the edge of the Montopolis* barrio *and a block or so from the African American cemetery. At the time, African Americans could not be buried in cemeteries reserved for Whites. I walked past that cemetery every day on my way to school.*

As part of the deal, the patrona *sold two old farm buildings to my father so that by tearing them down and salvaging the materials he could use them to build our new house. Tearing down buildings so that the materials can be reused is a very labor intensive affair. So the whole family got into the act. It is through that experience that I learned how to use a crowbar to take nails out of boards without wrecking them. Our family labor was augmented by one nonfamily volunteer:* Don *Medina. The term* don *is an honorific in Spanish that is usually applied to older men as a sign of respect. Normally the* don *is prefixed to the first name, but in this case, and for no apparent reason, the* don *was added to the last name.*

Since I was only 10 or 12 years old, Don *Medina seemed to me to be impossibly old. Most likely he was about 60 at the time. He had fought with the Carranza forces during the Mexican Revolution of 1910. I can still recall vividly the rivalry between* Don *Medina and* Don *Goyo, the labor contractor who had fought on the side of Pancho Villa. I eagerly absorbed the war stories that they told, wounds and all. It was only many years later that I recognized the great irony of two migrant workers in the fields of Michigan still sparring over a decades-old revolution that had long since turned into an institutional revolution of private gain and public corruption.*

Don *Medina worked on our house-building project without pay. He worked slowly, as older men tend to do, but steadily and without effort. He ate his meals with the rest of the family, and that was it. Actually, there was one more thing. Every Sunday, without exception,* Don *Medina could be seen walking on the gravel street coming from his house to visit us. He came to visit just before the noon meal. Now, the Sunday main meal was always a special affair at our house. You could always count on something like chicken* mole*, caldo de rez, and even enchiladas, which no one could possibly make better than my mother.* Don *Medina's perpetual Sunday visits clearly were designed to include the Sunday meal. Thus, through* Don *Medina's presence, the Sunday meal became a semipublic event at our house.*

Don Medina's story helps us to see how subtle and intricate the connections can be between the public and the private spheres. Contributing his labor to what was clearly a private house-building enterprise, *Don* Medina thereby gained acceptance to the Sunday meal, which normally would have been a private affair for the family. From *Don* Medina's perspective, he was contributing his labor to the public good of helping our family build a house. But through this action in the public arena, he was able to reshape the otherwise private Sunday meal at our house into a semipublic event.

Both of the stories that I have told include food as a theme. In some ways, talking about food is a very good way to explore the meaning of the public and the private, as well as their relationship. There can be little doubt that some aspects of food and eating are very private. After all, you can eat only with your own mouth, and usually you eat to keep your own body going. Yet, food almost always involves a public effort in getting the food and preparing it. In food there is always the issue of effort and ownership. There is the feeling that those who want to eat need to work for it, and that those who work are deserving of food. Food thus becomes a public good that ends up in private hands and stomachs. The thorny issue is how to get the food, prepare it, and distribute it equitably among individuals. Food reminds us of the fundamental need to deal with the public good and its connections to our most private desires and needs.

Pecans

Several years after we arrived in the United States, our family joined the stream of migrant workers who, like salmon about to spawn, found their way back to the fields of the great Midwest. The migrants left behind the hot and dusty border towns of south Texas as they moved northward in small and large trucks covered with canvas tarps or in used cars with small trailers behind them. For us, the destination was Michigan and every state in between. One of the inevitable consequences of this peripatetic lifestyle was that often we would have to leave school early or start school late. And so it was one fateful year when I transitioned from the relatively safe enclave of Allison Elementary School to the big junior high school outside of our familiar barrio. *I started several weeks late into the first grading period. But as usual, I approached my studies energetically so that I could catch up as quickly as possible. But this time, in seventh grade, everything was really different.*

The school had a number of large pecan trees on its property. As it turned out, harvesting the fruit of these trees was a fundraising activity for the school. But then somebody had to pick the pecans, a labor-intensive activity if there ever was one. The solution was to allow various classes to go out and pick pecans for a class period instead of attending to their regular studies. To give things a semblance of noncoercion, the teacher of the designated class would ask the students if they preferred to do classwork or pick pecans for that class period. Naturally, almost all of the students eagerly consented to pick pecans. But not me. What an absurdity! I had been picking crops all summer long. I had missed school. And

now that I was desperately trying to catch up on missed schoolwork I was sup-
posed to go out and pick pecans instead! So I raised my hand and told the teacher
no. Not only that, I told her that I was in school to learn, and that picking pecans
was not my idea of learning.

Well, that was it for the 20-something White school teacher who I am con-
vinced must have believed that what we Mexicans needed most was strong disci-
pline. She ran her class like a boot camp. Since we had already had a similar
difference of opinion before, she was convinced that I was a troublemaker and
sent me off to the principal's office. I had never been to a principal's office before
on a disciplinary matter. But there I was. The principal was an ex-Navy man
who looked remarkably like a bulldog. He wore his hair in a flattop, as was
popular in those days. Even though he was still young, his cheeks and jowls hung
from his face as in someone who has had plenty to eat. But it also gave him the
look of an attack dog, something he might even have cultivated with the students.
I think that he, too, must have believed that discipline is what Mexicans needed
most. He gave me a severe tongue lashing and threatened me with a belt whip-
ping if I did not straighten out. I was not afraid of him. But I was beside myself
with fury and an absolute feeling of impotence. I did not really hear what he had
to say. Tears streamed from my eyes, not out of fear, but from the sheer rage,
helplessness, and even shame that I was feeling for being talked to that way. It
was an involuntary reaction. And all the while I could see myself, the situation I
was in, and my reaction to it as if I were an observer watching a scene. Needless
to say, it was a perfect example of a lesson learned organically.

From the school's point of view, I am sure that having the students pick
pecans instead of doing classwork was a contribution to the public good of
the school. But for me, at that moment, picking pecans instead of attending
to my studies was a severe deprivation of my private good—of my desire to
learn and do well in school, and of my dream to make something of myself.
In promoting the public good, it is necessary to look carefully to see whose
ox is being gored in the interest of the greater good, for the public good
cannot really be promoted at the expense of competing and legitimate public
or private interests. Those whose oxen are gored for the public good should
at least expect to receive some compensation for their losses. Like everything
else, the public good is almost always based on someone's frame of reference.
This frame of reference can include unearned privileges and unfair exclu-

sions, so we should not just resort to the belt to sanction the public good. We ought to consider that the private good is not always insolent or evil.

In the pecan story, my private good of doing well in school was overwhelmed by the public good of raising money for the school. It was my desire to become an educated person that received a thrashing that day. But underneath it all, it was my objection, my public protest, that upset the young teacher. Even though we were very young, some of us already knew that things were not right with our education. We also were willing to stand up and challenge the system. Normally, it is the parents' role to challenge the system on behalf of their children. In our case, our parents did indeed speak for us, but they spoke for us through our very own mouths and tongues. They did so because of the organic lessons they had taught us about what is right and wrong. Meanwhile our erstwhile teachers and principals must have sensed that something was afoot; what they were sensing were the very early stirrings of *El Movimiento*. Some dozen years later, Chicana/o students, facing similar neglect by the schools, took to the streets, boycotted schools, and demanded a quality education. Their individual desires for a good education and a better life had somehow morphed into a public good. The instrument for vindicating that public good was *El Movimiento*, the Chicano Movement.

Valedictorian

I was a freshman at Oakland University in Rochester, Michigan, in the fall of 1964. Somehow I had managed to graduate from Fremont High School in western Michigan. I was the first in my family to graduate from high school. My older siblings, one at a time, had quit school to go to work and help out the family or strike out on their own. I should have taken the same path, but I was stubborn as a mule. I toughed it out on sheer determination and bottles of Maalox. I graduated as valedictorian.

But I was an interloper of sorts in that high school. By residence I should have attended Holton High School, which, in fact, I attended during my junior year. But Holton High School was easily one of the most impoverished schools in the state, and the quality of its instruction was hardly exemplary. So I went to see the superintendent of the Fremont schools and explained my desire to return to Fremont High School. Since I had the reputation of being a good student, the superintendent was sympathetic. He said that if I could get to a pickup point for the school bus, he would try to get someone to pay my tuition. He couldn't just let me cross district boundaries and run the risk of being accused of robbing the good students from the neighboring school district. He apparently found an anonymous donor who paid my tuition, and I was able to finish my senior year at Fremont High School.

The problem is that I had very good grades, but they were earned at three different schools. And the difference in grade point average between me and the next highest student was very small indeed. So that made selection of the valedictorian a real problem. Were they really going to give it to a migrant worker who couldn't even pay his own tuition? Weren't some of his grades suspect? I really don't know what must have gone on behind closed doors. I do know this: I was indeed designated as valedictorian. However, there was no valedictory speech that year. I was not invited to give one. Instead, as I walked the stage to receive my diploma and shake the superintendent's hand, it was announced, "Raymond Padilla, valedictorian." That was good enough for me. My parents were in the audience, the only time they had ever set foot in that school.

Like the two strands in DNA, the private and the public good are forever entwined in a spiraling embrace. Fulfilling my private desire for a good education depended on someone's willingness to enhance the public good, in this case educating a needy student. The act of compassion had to remain anonymous. Sometimes the public good is promoted in very private ways. But my good fortune resulted in some other deserving student not becoming the valedictorian of my class. By enhancing the public good, the anonymous donor had gored the hopes and dreams of another student. Somehow a compromise was worked out. I came out the winner, not just because of my hard work, but also because of the willingness of others to enhance the public good. The anonymous donor, the superintendent, those who decided who would be valedictorian, none of them belonged to my own ethnic group. Yet, on the whole, they treated me well. I learned that all groups have the capacity to promote the public good, and that there are individuals in every group who will always opt for the private good. The private and the public good are almost always in tension. We make choices, and those choices give shape to our lives and, indeed, shape the very society in which we live.

Carlos

Carlos was my friend. I first met him in 1970 when I was hired as the first Chicano admissions counselor at the University of Michigan, shortly after I received my bachelor's degree. Carlos was a financial aid officer at Eastern Michigan University, which is just down the street from the University of Michigan campus in Ann Arbor. Carlos was friendly, cheerful, and extremely energetic. His theme song was Don Quixote's "Impossible Dream." He was half a generation older than I and, as I soon found out, had quite a past. Most notably, he was an ex-convict, having spent a decade in prison for a felonious crime. He made no bones about it; he let you know about his past right away. I suppose he did not want that biographical detail to get in the way of things. He also had a master's degree in business administration, which was quite an accomplishment for a Chicano of his generation. He enjoyed the good life. Every day was a gift for him, and he tried to make the most of it. He drove a Cadillac, dressed impeccably in a suit and tie, and was almost always smoking a cigar. Invariably, he was in the vicinity of good food and drink and attractive women. How could you not like this guy?

Carlos and I and several others founded a new organization in Michigan, called the Association of Chicanos for College Admissions (ACCA). The acronym was intended to be suggestive; our logo was a clenched fist holding a bundle of pencils. Chicana/os of the movimiento *co-opted icons on a world scale, always adapting them to our needs. Not that there was any particular ideology tied to this organization. Our goal simply was to increase the number of Chicanas and Chicanos in college. It was through this organization and related activities that I first entered the world of activism in academia, my shot at promoting the public good. I took a leadership role in the organization, with Carlos as a trusted friend. There was never any competition with Carlos for formal leadership in these types of organizations. Perhaps because of his past, Carlos had decided to be the king maker rather then the king. So he exerted his influence, which was considerable, behind the scenes.*

What was there not to like about Carlos? For some people it was this: While he definitely promoted the public good, it was his modus operandi to almost always claim what might be called "his cut." Not that he necessarily did anything illegal or even improper. It's just that he would almost always seek ways to "maximize" his activities. That meant looking for ways to gain private benefits from promoting the public good. He was not secretive about this. It was plain to see that he would look for personal opportunities within the context of enhancing the public good. And he was very skilled at it. I quickly picked up on this behavior but I reasoned as follows. Is it necessarily the case that all promotion of the public good must entail some kind of personal sacrifice? Does proportion matter in terms of private versus public gain? Are we better off collectively by having people who give but also take as opposed to people who either give nothing or always only take? I concluded that sacrifice ought not to be made a necessary element of promoting the public good. Sometimes the public good can be enhanced by someone who also benefits privately. If the enhanced public good far exceeds the private gain, then so be it. Over the years, what really bothered me were those individuals who pretended to promote the public good but really were only out for themselves. Unlike Carlos, who was quite open about his private gain, these individuals conceal their true intentions and take on leadership roles, ostensibly to promote the public good, but they wind up only promoting themselves and their interests. These false leaders are called *vendidos, tio tacos*, coconuts, yo-yos, sell outs, and so on. The multiplicity of names should tell us that the phenomenon is not uncommon.

But I suppose that it's all a matter of degree. For all the strategizing to gain personal benefits, in the end Carlos contributed more to the public good than did his sanctimonious critics who most likely were jealous of his success. He took some but he gave much. There may be some who give much and take nothing, but they are much harder to come by. In the very real but imperfect world that we must live in, sometimes the public good can be enhanced only by people like Carlos. And we should not be too hasty to condemn them. Although Carlos was by no means a devil, the public good sometimes must dance with the devil, *con la cola entre las patas*. To dance with the devil is one thing, especially if you have not yet seen *la cola* and the goat's feet hidden underneath the suit. To go to bed with the devil is quite another. The art of promoting the public good is knowing how to distinguish between the two.

Ars Publica

When I started college in the fall of 1964, the Beat generation was still in vogue. Writers such as Jack Kerouac and poets such as Lawrence Ferlinghetti and Allen Ginsberg continued to be the literary icons for the bohemian set. The standard attire for the beatniks was motorcycle boots and denim, and beards were in. So, as a migrant worker and for the first time in my life, I was dressed for the occasion. I just needed to add the beard. Never mind that similarly clad freshmen arrived on campus in limousines or sports cars. I took a bus to Pontiac from my summer dish-washing job on Mackinaw Island, which took most of the night, and hitch-hiked the rest of the way to the Oakland University campus just in time to partici-pate in the last freshman orientation, which was mandatory. I had no idea that in a couple of years the beatniks would be transformed into the "hippies," those wild children of World War II veterans who decided to abandon the inner cities for the greener pastures of suburbia. It was the hippies, the flower children, who would launch the "counterculture" and give rise to "yippies," the politicized ver-sion of hippies. After the oil crises of 1973 and the end of the Vietnam War in 1974, these hippies and yippies and other counterculturalists would be transmogrified into "yuppies," that implacable herd of me-centered baby boomers who wanted it all for themselves and right now. It was a kind of reverse metamorphosis, the but-terfly turning into a nasty and ravenous worm. But all of that was in the future.

There is no doubt that in the fall of 1964 I felt an affinity toward beatniks. Perhaps it was their outsider status, maybe it was the fact that they were "cool" and "hip," or maybe it was their connection to the arts. At the time I was toying with the idea that I might be a poet. I was reading the Evergreen Review. *One day I looked at the front cover of the magazine and there it was, almost like a cartoon. It was a beatnik-type character confronting a very middle-class looking lady who was facing a painting. The balloon dialogue said something like, "Lady, don't appreciate art. Be art!" Be art! That emphatic phrase echoed in my head like a bell that would not stop ringing. What could that mean? What could that mean for me, the would-be poet? There had to be some important message encoded in those two words. Be art! I must figure it out!*

A few years later, the answer rolled over me like a giant tsunami. It was the Chicano Movement of the late '60s that provided a canvas large enough not just to produce art, but to be art. The key to being art is the public good. I suppose that the public good can be approached from many angles. For poli-ticians, the public good is a platform to stand on and win elections. For social workers, the public good is helping people out of their misery. For those with a religious bent, promoting the public good is a divinely inspired duty. For academics, the public good is what needs to be studied in order to understand it and use it wisely. But for me, the migrant and would-be poet, the *movimiento* as public good became a medium not for producing art but for being art.

The *movimiento* was pure energy, human energy unleashed after generations of being bound and gagged. But that boundless, unchained energy
needed to be shaped and directed. It needed to be harmonized, harnessed,
and sculpted into constructions of the public good. The art of the public
good had to be seen as a performance, not a representation. To be art is to be
present. To be art is to be active in real time, fashioning collective action into
structures of the public good. The artist who is being art works with people
and institutions as the artistic medium. What people bring with them are
their dreams, desires, and passions. Also their misery, pain, and suffering. Not
to mention their greed, egotism, and lust for power. But all of these elements
require artistry if anything resembling the public good is to be constructed
from them. So in my mid-20s I decided not to become an artist who produces
representational art but an artist who strives to be art, and in doing so I bet
my future on learning how to master the art of the public good.

What is remarkable is how my innermost feelings and desires, my private
world, became enmeshed in the art of the public good. But combining my
private good with the public good did not occur in a simple additive fashion.
It was more like a squaring of the private good and a squaring of the public
good, which, when added together, produced social and institutional
changes that materially affected people's lives. From this I also learned that
the public good is not likely to materialize as a social reality unless someone
is willing to be art.

To be art, then, is the true cost of the public good. As I think now about
that Beat artist rebuking the lady who was appreciating art, it may well be
that what the Beat artist was trying to say is that there is a cost to being art.
Unless one is willing to pay the price and be art, there can be only representational art, art that can be appreciated but not lived. The *movimiento* made
it possible for me to be an artist and to be art while promoting the public
good. From this experience, I learned that the public good as art is a sym-
phony that must be performed with people's lives as instruments, a poem
that must be lived, and a sculpture that must come to life.

Reference

González, M. C. (1995). In search of the voice I always had. In R. V. Padilla &
R. C. Chávez (Eds.), *The leaning ivory tower. Latino professors in American universities* (pp. 77–90). Albany: State University of New York Press.

JENNIFER AYALA

3

VOCES IN DIALOGUE
What Is Our Work in the Academy?

Jennifer Ayala

If you ask me who I am,
I'll tell you
LATINA.
Cubana y Ecuatoriana.
Nuyorkina-born, Jersey raised.
A daughter of diasporas-meeting-at-the-borderlands,
learning to speak the tongues of tradition and creation:
Spanglish, English, Español, Académe.
I am a *madrina*, sister, partner, (re)searcher,
knowledge facilitator, eternal student, recent *doctora*.
I am many voices . . .

I am many voices; some sing, some scold, some whisper. Each voice, a note in my biography, narrates a different understanding of what my/ our work is in higher education. My growing up years, *mi familia*, my experiences in a progressive graduate school program, my research, my journeys as an academic and administrator in public and private colleges, all reshape my vision of higher education. In this piece, I slide between poetry and prose as I grapple with what these multiple voices and interpretations tell me about my place and mission within a system of education penetrated by corporate interests, shifting funding priorities, as well as pockets of action, possibility, and transformation. Throughout my experiences, I learned that my mission is about connection, community, reintegrating imposed ruptures and fragmentations, a feeling of wholeness (see also Lara, 2000).

Growing Up with *el Baile de Biculturalism*

Growing up in a river of multiplicities, my biculturality was a skill of fluidity I caught onto early. This meant that I knew I had to use *usted* and *señora* to the Ecuadorian side of my family, switch to a Cuban pitch (a few decibels louder) to be heard among my mother's side of the family, speak proper English in classrooms (though this was a later lesson), and a hybrid blend of English and Spanish with one group of friends. Even though I was born in the United States, my first language was Spanish. Spanish and school were not exclusive of each other at first. Half the class was spent speaking and learning in Spanish and the other half was in English. This experience reminds me of the more harmonious moments of the multiplicity and biculturality I lived with early on. Home and school voices were both allowed in the classroom.

Reminiscing about the days of my childhood in Queens, I have fond, vivid memories.

> My childhood smells like fresh rain on the pavement,
> And sounds like the roar of the R train above
> And skin-scraping swirls of cement
> And smacks of sticks hitting *piñatas*
> With splashes of candy pouring down.
> Tastes of guava and merengue
> And of *buñuelos* golden brown.
> My childhood smells like fresh rain on the pavement
> where I live between generations
> And *abuela* would watch over me
> Along with the other neighborhood kids.
> Some nights I joined my parents
> cleaning office floors.
> During the day they worked
> and studied more
> eventually slipping through a middle-class door.
> My childhood smells like fresh rain on the pavement

where my feet are hushed at school
but I sneak games of wall ball on the street
where I'm called Jenifa by my friends
where kisses are exchanged for sweets
and a metal lunchbox was my weapon
and *Chespirito* was always on.
My childhood smells like fresh rain on the pavement
Where I dance, dream, imagine
Set aside Barbie
So I could peer into the secret passage,
A deep fissure between buildings perfectly aligned,
so that I see hints of orange from the setting sun,
a stream of noiseless cars zipping by on the run.
And imagine alternate universes
And tell *abuelo* monsters were my friends.
My childhood smells like fresh rain on the pavement
Where I feel snowflakes on my outstretched tongue
stretch my arms out to tomorrow,
cherish this time borrowed
touching yesterday's reflection
on the pools of water collecting
in the cracks on the pavement.

I guess you could say I was in the habit of using my imagination, as children do, to create my own alternate spaces of wonder and possibility.

My parents then got a "good job" in New Jersey and we all moved. In my new grammar school, students were allowed to run on the school grounds made of grass and trees instead of the swirls of concrete to which I had been accustomed. There were not as many Latinas/os in this particular school. Speaking Spanish in the classroom or among friends was now considered inappropriate, rude, a marker of difference, possibly a sign that I might encounter academic or behavioral difficulties. It was here that I first heard the word "Spic." I became very shy in school but forged friendships with White and the few Latina and Asian girls in my class. In settings like this, we (Latinas, and girls of color in general) tended to find each other, seek one another out. In high school, these groups solidified into different cliques that I belonged to—a group of White friends and a Latina group. I felt generally supported by my teachers, particularly, maybe amazingly, English teachers, who encouraged me to write and express myself creatively. They helped push my writing and thinking, so that I felt prepared for this aspect of college. But I came to understand that aspects of myself needed to be kept separate: who I was at school, with my Latina/o group of friends, with my White group of friends, with my *familia*. I learned the codes appropriate to each group and could slip and slide between them if/when I chose to. But I wonder . . .

> Am I like
> fading footprints in the snow
> that melt and transform
> to a still water
> who changes shape
> according to what holds me,
> what surrounds me?

I also discovered thin lines of intersection, spaces where bridges could be forged between the worlds I kept separate (Anzaldua, 1987). Sometimes I danced around that thin line, sometimes I felt I was that thin line between.

Cancion Mestiza

With this understanding, with biculturality and code-switching as skills, with multiplicity and hybridity as my mainstream, I became adept at finding communities of support. In my school and work experiences, I learned how to create community across multiplicities and to find key allies. For example, in graduate school, though I formed a more lasting, othermother relationship with one mentor in particular, I had multiple advisors. I drew upon the experiences of each, working with and flowing (well, not always flowing) between them, based on their unique frameworks. This, however, was not always easy to accomplish.

Graduate school was a place where I felt there was a space for me to integrate more of the home and academic voices I had learned so well to keep separate. Thin line expanding, my voices of home were opened up in the classroom once again to inform and speak to the social science academic. Martin-Baro's (1994) liberation psychology welcomed me to the program. I could write and research with/about Latinas/os, something I had begun to do in my final years of college, use Spanglish in my academic writing, and position myself within the work I did. I was disappointed that there weren't more students or faculty of color at the time, but I loved the radical spirit that lives here, the committed mentors, the tight community cohort of students. Many of my classmates did not fit the traditional graduate student mold and trajectory. Some were activists, most were committed to the betterment of their communities and the applied action potential of research. Here was a "free space" where I was encouraged to find/express my voice of social critique in a community of critical consciousness.

> I am a witness to/perpetrator of violence,
> Oppression's stepchild.
> Seen many of its faces,
> On the outside,
> as the isms that bleed us,
> through policies that exclude us
> and shout
> "Go home. You don't belong. You don't deserve."
> In structures that move the clouds to our skies
> so the sun can shine on theirs.[1]
> But on the inside, where the shadows are cast,
> we often drink the poisoned rain,
> and spit it on each other,
> bruising the face,
> tearing the flesh,
> killing the spirit
> of too many in our communities . . .

There was a place for me to discuss social injustices and critique structural arrangements that erupt as public and private violences. The private violences taking the form of domestic violence, internalized racism, the ways we wound one another. And the public violences highlight the private, to hide its role in perpetuating them through structural inequalities and social injustice (Lara, 2002). I learned other languages to speak about issues of social justice: critical race theory, queer theory, feminist/womanist understandings, decolonizing methodologies. I reflected more explicitly on the injustices that exist and on the power we have to disrupt and/or reproduce them. My learning happened in a collective of spaces inside and outside the classroom. It happened in a huddle of program peers, in offices, faculty living rooms

---

[1] This line was inspired by a poetry slam poet.

and kitchens, in seats on subway cars, in local dives, and in studying lives; I learned and lived a critical education.

Research was viewed critically for its mis/use as social reproduction and its potential to be a tool for and with communities, as action, as interruption of hegemony and structural inequality. The civic mission modeled for me here was the struggle toward action for/with communities through research. I say struggle because lots of times we did not get it right, but there was a movement and a commitment to it among many faculty and students. Prepared with tools of research and frames of inquiry, I had the opportunity to work with activist organizations. I learned much from them, and from these experiences in general I learned that I could use research to advance social justice goals.

It was in these graduate school years that I also was introduced to a powerful experience in teaching. The course was an East Coast/West Coast collaboration, codeveloped and cotaught between Latina graduate student instructors and a Latina health organization (Ayala, Herrera, Jimenez, & Lara, 2006). I was introduced to the intersection between academic and spirit work. Spirit as an open understanding, as emotional awakening, as a faith within, as a connection to people and the earth, and not an imposition of any particular religious ideology, though it could be that for some (see also Avila, 1999; Castillo, 1994). Grounded in a philosophy of an integrated bodymindspirit (Lara, 2002), interdisciplinary intellectual/critical, community, and emotional/spirit work was deeply embedded into the class. Inside the classroom, we had creative projects, team teaching, nonacademic local knowledge holders as speakers, class discussions, check-ins, and sessions. Connecting to outside the class, the course involved direct service work with community-based organizations; creating reproductive health conferences with students, housed in the academy but inviting and targeting the local community; and healing work with interested students using a variation of talking circles. Between classes, the co-instructors and I would engage in intense collaborative planning and the spirit work of sessioning. This work was a unique way of teaching for me. It was teaching as transgression, teaching toward personal and collective transformation (hooks, 1994). I felt I was serving a role in fulfilling a civic mission, and that I was being served by one as well. But it was not easy work. The vulnerability that often accompanies this type of work, vulnerability in the eyes of academia and in the eyes of some students, was a tremendous challenge (see Ayala et al., 2006).

I am still working on incorporating more of my voices into the work I do. As Anzaldua (Moraga & Anzaldua, 1983, 1987) taught me, code-switching does not have to be just a personal strategy of moving between different worlds that need to be kept separate. It should be an act of constructing bridges between them, having the voices intermingle, disturbing the harmony to make a more meaningful rhythm. It is *una cancion mestiza* (Anzaldua, 1987). I have witnessed models of education that interrupt undeserved hierarchies and oppressive dichotomies. With my third eye, I could see the possibility of working in an alternate space of multiplicities (Anzaldua, 1987) and co-construct classroom community here.

Voces of Doubt

These experiences helped me think about teaching and research as social justice work, as healing fragmentations, as collaboration with community, as bridge work. As I try to enact a vision, formulate a way of knowing, trust what is within me and around me, I feel a surge of interruptions from voices of doubt.

> Say something! You don't have anything profound enough to say. Is this rigorous enough? Does it meet the standards? Is it transformative, critical work? So what? How will this help get me a job? Stop hand-holding. You're not guiding enough. Too political. Not political enough. You're imposing your liberal views on me. You're selling out. You're not giving back enough. Remember who you are. Stop flaunting who you are as decoration. Act the way we think you should. It's too much! But you're just not enough . . .

The voices of doubt narrate a tale of inadequacy and visit me every time I teach, with every new project I undertake, with every student I advise. They were always there. In graduate school, at first I could not help feeling like I wasn't good enough, sharp enough, critical enough, well-written enough, smart enough to be a student in this program. I was a fraud, and it was just a matter of time before I would be found out. It took a while before I was confident enough to feel like I might in fact belong. When I cotaught the Latina health class, I would often be overrun with emotion because I doubted my own legitimacy as a teacher. Now that I am on the other side of the imaginary divide between student and faculty, I still find myself doubting my own teaching abilities and worthiness. Some of the critical perspectives that seemed welcomed in my graduate school life did not necessarily transfer well into other academic settings. I seem to hold back some of my ideas in certain settings, even the classroom. This is a self-imposed restriction by my *voces* of doubt. In a time/place where there is a strong voice of conservative thought, I try to create an atmosphere of inquiry, without consciously imposing my own views. This is something I struggle with a lot. On the one hand, the dominant voice gets a lot of airtime, and it is important to understand multiple perspectives and challenge strongly held truths. In an atmosphere of questioning and debate, I want students to come up with their own ideas, even if I really don't like their conclusions. And there are times when I deeply disagree with their conclusions. I take to heart student concerns that coursework should help them in their search for employment. Higher education is no longer a "luxury" of learning, consciousness raising, and personal growth but a way in which to achieve social mobility. But are these really luxuries? Is what's being asked of me by some (education as job training) really going to help with social mobility? I strongly believe in the transformative power/function of higher education and must also consider these needs in the context of the search for economic power/independence. Why do I find myself always creating a binary out of these goals? Yes, the voices of doubt are ever present, but they can be informative and propel me to rethink my assumptions and continue to question, and change.

Clashes of Mission and System Realities

There is an existing and sometimes overpowering "system" voice that speaks of education as standardization and corporatization. We see it taking hold in K–12 education, but also increasingly in higher education, as authors Aronowitz (2000), Bok (2003), and Kirp (2003), among others, are writing. Corporatization trends manifest themselves in how colleges describe themselves, project their public images, frame students and staff/faculty work. Students are our customers, corporations are buying/owning university research labs (and sometimes their findings), and corporate consultants are being called upon to shape various departments (Bok, 2003; Kirp, 2003). Standardization is reaching into the college arena; perhaps it has always been there. Our department recently had to retool all the syllabi so that they are aligned with state-determined standards. Weekly department meetings consist of trying to decipher what accrediting agencies are looking for. Undergoing national accreditation and reaccreditation processes means understanding what it means to create and implement imposed standards.

> The game of standards.
> Here's how you play:
> We tell you
> To make your own
> But, you understand
> we mean make them look like us.

At one point, we were reminded that this process was to hold us accountable to measurable standards we as a department deem important in educating students. We are to create our own definitions of success. However, when our department decided against using a standardized test score as one measure of success, we were reminded that it was essential to include that measure if we wanted to strengthen our chances of reaccreditation. We discussed the possibility of fighting this, but the reality is, without this formalized seal of approval our department would dissolve.

Engaging students in transformative work with communities, committing to social justice, enjoying student diversity, advocating for the rights of all students are not necessarily recognized as institutional strengths. On a smaller scale, some departments at the uniquely ethnically and economically diverse college in which I currently work have historically been very committed to the students. In fact, rapport with students is an important quality sought after in faculty, sometimes considered over research and publication experience. This has had consequences in terms of the tenure and promotion process of some faculty. Typically, rapport with students and student advocacy in many higher education institutions takes second place, if any place at all, in the reward structure of higher education.

On a larger scale, reputable colleges are often defined, at least in part, by the degree of exclusion they practice: how many students are rejected, how many low-SAT-scoring individuals they were able to keep out so as to boast a high SAT profile. Second chances for motivated but academically struggling students are indicators that a college does not hold high standards. Colleges whose mission and reality is to educate students with diverse academic, ethnic, cultural, class, ideological profiles may not always be considered "highly ranked" in the market of higher education. In these popular college rankings, there is no serious measure of diversity and/or commitment to social justice work. More often, having significant diversity means that the college's rigor and reputation are held suspect. Colleges, particularly small colleges, that may choose to run counter to these trends can find themselves struggling for survival in the market of higher education. National recognition and reputation are not often (or ever?) based on commitment to civic mission and the public good. Ultimately, then, we must ask whose public and whose good. At some colleges, framings of public good may focus on communities of "other" but not those housed within its walls. Students with great desires but great needs are also a community that should be recognized as a "worthy" public.

This has implications for the civic mission of colleges; to survive, will missions be recast, couched in a market-friendly framework? This is a potentially significant challenge to missions and works that are for the public good.

The Third Eye: Looking Now and Ahead

I am reminded that I am strongest when in community with others. Perhaps that is my/our work in the academy: the forging of healing connections among the community, academy, ourselves as an indivisible bodymindspirit (Lara, 2002). In teaching, I found disruption and healing work with the Latina health experience and, in research, with the approaches and issues that we engaged. It was the totality of that work that I felt; here, this is mission. Growing up, I moved with my multiplicities and learned the values of living within and between social worlds of home, school, and different peer groups—precursors to bridging and forging third-space communities. With the class, we crossed disciplinary borders and hierarchical arrangements, created community with team teaching, and engaged as a community with some critical, if painful, topics and issues. In graduate school and beyond, I found such a space in the kind of research that does not seek to understand in order to reinforce hegemonic practices.

Participatory action research is one such potential home because it invites community/academic collaborations. Because the knowledge, at once shaped and informed by community, can become a tool through which voices can be amplified and action can be taken. From this collaboration can emerge a collection of possibilities with action and products such as spoken-word performances, DVDs, websites, books, dance, theater (see Fine and colleagues, 2003, 2004). This is where the academic sings the *cancion mestiza*, piercing through the divides between mission and reality.

Many times I wonder what I am doing to respond to the civic mission of higher education. My current academic home is founded on the Jesuit tradition of a social-justice-oriented mission, one that involves embracing and serving the local urban community. I feel it in advising students experiencing academic difficulty, in brainstorming with colleagues on micro and macro issues of social justice ranging from antiwar efforts, to campus activities that promote our civic mission, to individual student concerns. I see it around me in the work of my colleagues to vigorously advocate for students' rights or even just invite students to their homes for dinner. But I often feel this is not enough.

Most recently, collaborating across disciplines and campuses with a power core of committed colleagues, I am feeling a revival of mission through research. We are working on action research projects with student and community-based collaboratives. This is classroom work, academic work, but also community and spirit work with students. One project involves working with a small group of freshmen on an action research project with a local after-school program that serves children in the community. Part of the research involves direct service to the organization. On the first day our small group was to visit the organization together, a number of unfamiliar faces joined us. They were not part of this class but simply had heard of the opportunity and wanted to tag along just to see if they could volunteer their time at this site, following their own civic mission. They were not looking for money or academic credit, just hungering for the opportunity to make a difference in their community. This is academic work because it involves writing and reading, systematic observation, training and use of research methods, library research, analyzing, reporting, public speaking. It is community work, not only because of the direct service, but also because the nature of the research is sought by and intended for the organization with which we are working. It is spirit work because this type of collaboration blurs the boundaries between community and academy, where the organization is enriching all of us in return with its insights and work with us (part of their mission to the community), and because this collaboration is integrating our different selves, fulfilling a sense of wholeness and connection. In speaking to social and community workers, Lila Watson, a Brisbane-based aboriginal activist, said, "our liberation is bound up together."

To me, serving the public means educating all of our students. Serving the public means opening the borders of the academy to the community. Serving the public means engaging students with community work through cooperative modes of investigation. It means questioning, stirring curiosity, engaging the bodymindspirit, creating borderlands in the classroom, working with students and other college staff partners as community bridges, singing the *cancion mestiza*, transforming and allowing ourselves to be transformed.

> With sisters, brothers, allies
> I am/we are actors,
> together a Force.
> We sift through the injustices,
> so long draped in collective silence,
> and solder the fragments,
> piece by piece,
> with our *deseos* and *sueños*,
> our *respeto* and love,
> our spirits and communities strong.
> Such is the journey healing.

References

Anzaldua, G. (1987). *Borderlands: The new Mestiza*. San Francisco: Aunte Lute Press.

Aronowitz, S. (2000). *The knowledge factory: Dismantling the corporate university and creating true higher learning*. Boston: Beacon Press.

Avila, E. (1999). In the beginning. In E. Avila & J. Parker, *Woman who glows in the dark: A curandera reveals traditional Aztec secrets of physical and spiritual health* (pp. 15–39). New York: Putnam.

Ayala, J., Herrera, P., Jimenez, L., & Lara, I. (2006). *Fiera, guambra y karichina! Transgressing the borders of community and academy. In D. Delgado Bernal, C. A. Elenes, F. E. Godinez, & S. Villenas (Eds.), *Chicana/Latina education in everyday Life: Feminista perspectives on pedagogy and epistemology* (pp. 161–180). Albany: State University of New York Press.

Bok, D. (2003). *Universities in the Marketplace: The Commercialization of Higher Education*. Princeton, NJ: Princeton University Press.

Castillo, A. (1994). Brujas and curanderas: A Lived Spirituality. In A. Castillo, *Mas-*

sacre of the Dreamers: Essays on Xicanismo (pp. 145–161). Albuquerque: University of New Mexico.

Fine, M., Roberts, R., Torre, M. E., Bloom, J., Burns, A., Chajet, L., Guishard, M., & Payne, Y. (2004). *Echoes: Youth documenting and performing the legacy of Brown vs. Board of Education.* New York: Teachers College Press.

Fine, M., Torre, M. E., Boudin, K., Bowen, I., Clark, J., Hylton, D., Martinez, M. "Missy," Roberts, R. A., Smart, P., & Upegui, D. (2003). Participatory Action Research: From within and beyond prison bars. In P. Camic, J. E. Rhodes, & L. Yardley (Eds.), *Qualitative research in psychology: Expanding perspectives in methodology and design* (pp. 173–198). Washington, DC: American Psychological Association.

hooks, b. (1994). *Teaching to transgress: Education as the practice of freedom.* New York: Routledge.

Kirp, D. L. (2003). *Shakespeare, Einstein, and the bottom line: The marketing of higher education.* Cambridge, MA: Harvard University Press.

Lara, I. (2002). Healing suenos for academia. In G. Anzaldua & A. Keating (Eds.), *This bridge we call home: Radical visions for transformation* (pp. 433–438). New York: Routledge.

Martin-Baro, I. (1994). *Writings for a liberation psychology.* Cambridge, MA: Harvard University Press.

Moraga, C., & Anzaldua, G. (1983). *This bridge called my back: Writings by radical women of color.* New York: Kitchen Table: Women of Color Press.

AÍDA HURTADO

ARCELIA L. HURTADO

MARÍA A. HURTADO

4

TRES HERMANAS (THREE SISTERS)

A Model of Relational Achievement

Aída Hurtado, María A. Hurtado, and Arcelia L. Hurtado

We are three *hermanas* (sisters). As the oldest, I am respectively 11 years and 18 older than my two younger sisters. We grew up in three cities—Tampico and Reynosa in Tamaulipas, Mexico, and McAllen in southern Texas—it seems that everything in our lives happens in trilogies.

Although we had a typical Mexican upbringing, my family is only nominally Catholic. We are one of many transnational families that are currently causing the furor among anti-immigrant activists. Like other immigrant families, our parents crossed the border into the United States primarily to provide their children with educational opportunities that were not available in Mexico. Our family moved from the hustle and bustle of Tampico, one of Mexico's most beautiful (at least in our eyes) cities, to the dusty, provincial, and backward (again, in our eyes) border town of Reynosa. The three sisters lived for various amounts of time in Tampico, Reynosa, and McAllen before our sojourn into higher education and, ultimately, into our respective and very different professions. So *las tres hermanitas* (not to be confused with the children's story of the three little pigs [also, three siblings], although like all good *mexicanas*, we tend toward the chunky side) tell their stories and reflect on why we chose careers for the public good.

From left to right, Arcelia, Aída, and María Hurtado

Hermana Número Uno: Aída,[1] aka *Chata, Chatosqui-Zabludovsky,*[2] ____ Fill in the Blank

I was *número uno* in the family in several respects: the first granddaughter of the eldest and most-favored daughter on my mother's side and the first child

---

[1] I am the namesake of my mother's middle sister, who was named after the "Triumphant March of Aída," a piece from Verdi's opera of the same name. While my family did not listen to opera, the "Triumphant March" is played to introduce young women turning 15 into society during the Mexican celebration called *quinceañera*. Most Mexican families are very familiar with this majestic piece of music.

[2] This nickname is based on the rhyming of my nickname and Jacobo Zabludovsky's last name. Jacobo Zabludovsky was a famous television and newspaper journalist in Mexico during the 1970s and 1980s. His television programs were similar to the U.S. programs *60 Minutes* and *Larry King Live*. Zabludovsky

of the most loving father any baby girl could possibly have. My special status was sanctified on my maternal grandfather's 1954 truck, which he christened *La Chata* in honor of my cherubic face punctuated by an unusually flat nose that everyone in the family referred to as *la fresa* (the strawberry).

During my early childhood in Tampico, until the age of six, I lived with various family members, depending on my parents' jobs. Both of my parents came from families complicated by various common-law marriages, adoptions (informal), and other life circumstances. It would take a dissertation to explain the relationships in a single household, let alone those in the 8 to 10 households (depending on how you define "household") in which I lived. My early life is marked by fluidity among many caring adults; I never experienced boundaries based on the "nuclear family."

Although all of our family members were extremely poor, it was not a poverty that included deprivation—either in the basic needs of life, such as food, or in psychological terms, as I always felt loved. Ours was a chaotic family full of laughter, conversation, and, yes, high tempers. Because we hailed from a city on the Gulf of Mexico, we were more Caribbean than northern Mexican in our outlook. Tampico is one of the largest seaports in the country, endowed with a tropical climate, including extreme heat and humidity, and beautiful vegetation.

In situating my choice of profession as a *social* psychologist, I have dedicated myself to understanding why people are normal rather than analyzing why people are unhappy (as is typically done in clinical practice). I have always been intrigued by context (in my case, which country I happen to live in) and how it makes one feel accepted and loved or scrutinized and excluded. I came to understand very early in life that happiness and well-being were dependent on context—that dispositional characteristics change depending on the social context. I also came to learn how necessary it was to be engaged beyond the nuclear family to be a happy and well-functioning adult. In other words, our collective public good was intimately tied to our individual happiness.

Why Education? Why Public Service?

As Lorna Dee Cervantes poignantly writes, "I come from a long line of eloquent illiterates whose history reveals what words don't say" (quoted in Sán-

---

was as well known in Mexico and the rest of Latin America as are U.S. journalists Dan Rather, Ted Koppel, Mike Wallace, and Larry King.

chez, 1988, pp. 17, 29). In my case, not one family member on either side had attended higher education in the United States before me. My father dropped out of school after third grade, and his mother did not know how to read or write (he never knew his father). However, my grandmother became a successful businesswoman by selling tacos at the *mercado* (marketplace) in Tampico, close to the port where ships from all over the world were docked. In addition, she was a *comercianta* (merchant) traveling to other parts of Mexico (mostly San Luis Potosi and Mexico City) to buy linens, fresh flowers, and other *chucherias* (knickknacks) for resale. As she became savvier in business, she even traveled to McAllen, Texas (before we moved there), to buy U.S. goods, mostly from the "Five-and-Ten" stores. Her house, which she bought and paid for through these commercial endeavors, was covered with this merchandise, which the neighbors often came over to admire (much like the household that Sandra Cisneros describes in her latest novel, *Caramelo* [2002]).

My grandmother loved to haggle over prices and asked my uncle—who was a caterer, florist, party planner (long before such a word existed), and, yes, openly gay—to keep long lists of all her clients' accounts. As a child and young adult, I especially liked *dia de los muertos* (Day of the Dead) because my uncle would make *coronas* (wreaths) out of crepe paper and fake flowers that we dipped in wax. My grandmother also sold *mondongo* (otherwise known as *menudo*, or "breakfast of champions," cow tripe soup) every Sunday *para la cruda* (for hangovers). We would set up several tables on the *banqueta* (sidewalk) outside her house where all the local *borrachitos* (little drunks who lived on the streets) and dockworkers would gather on Sunday mornings after their *parrandas* (partying) Saturday night. I was never bored when I stayed with my grandmother and her three grown children who, for various reasons, lived with her. Eventually my grandmother added a second floor onto her modest house for her youngest son (20 years my father's junior), who married and had four children of his own), and a third floor for her middle son (10 years my father's junior and who lived with his gay lover). Until her death at 94, my great-grandmother also lived with my grandmother. In this vital setting, I learned about flowers, travel, business, relationships, cooking, and, most of all, about loving those around you and helping those who come to your door. My grandmother's house was the hub of the neighborhood; I cannot remember a single day when the door was locked or when people did not stop by for business, conversation, and camaraderie.

My mother's father also did not go beyond an elementary school education. For a living, he painted houses and specialized in *rotulos*—elaborate signs that most commercial establishments required before the advent of computers. My grandfather's business was highly dependent on his gift of gab, as he had to "sell" his skills to prospective clients. One story in particular was often told within the family. My grandfather wanted to paint an affluent family's house. When he showed his paint samples to the potential client, he was told that one of his competitors was asking only half the price my grandfather was quoting. With a grand gesture of his hand and in a loud, booming voice, my grandfather, who never left the house without his fedora, responded, *"Pero señor, el no le ofrece lo último en pinturas para casas—El preparacote!"* (But sir, he doesn't offer you the latest in house paints—The Preparecoat!) He then explained that the *Preparacote* was de rigueur in house painting, sealing the paints to give the home brilliance and resistance to the hurricane winds that raged every year in the Gulf of Mexico. Needless to say, he got the job. The joke was that my grandfather had invented the word *Preparacote* and its capabilities on the spot. After a particularly good business deal, my grandfather would often offer money, food, and jobs to others; those around him generally knew him for his generosity, in particular, his extended family. He was the family member who insisted that my mother continue her schooling, even after her marriage to my father and her pregnancy with me. He paid for her books and uniform so that she could graduate, and she did so with honors. My mom was the first student ever to attend Tampico's nursing school while pregnant—this was back in 1952. Education, in the broadest sense of the word, was my grandfather's passion. Every night we would listen to the radio quiz shows together, learning geographical facts ("What is the capital of Russia?"—the announcer would query), great books in literature ("Who wrote *Hamlet?*" the announcer would continue), and the latest debates in politics ("Which politician steals the most public money? Too many to name!" the announcer would then quip, followed by a hearty laugh). I knew about Paris and the world before I left Tampico at the age of six.

My grandmother on my mother's side never attended school and never worked outside the home. She was from *la huasteca* (an indigenous region) in Veracruz, the neighboring state to Tamaulipas where Tampico is located.

She taught me several *huasteca* words and, from what I gathered many years later, probably was an indigenous person herself. Unlike my grandfather, who was *güero* (extremely light skinned with hazel eyes), my grandmother was dark skinned with piercing dark brown eyes and a temper to match. She could cook like no one I have ever met—a person who comes to mind is the fictitious Nacha in the novel *Como Agua Para Chocolate* (*Like Water for Chocolate* [Esquivel, 1992]). Days at her house began with a trip to *el mercado* to buy everything fresh for lunch, the main meal in Mexico. She never knew what she was going to prepare until she saw what was available at the open market, with food often coming in from all parts of the world. After the big meal at 1:00 in the afternoon, all businesses in Tampico would close down until 3:00, then reopen until 8:00 in the evening. This was my *amá* Chencha's time, which she generously shared with me. Fully clothed, we would climb into bed and read the two rival newspapers, *El Mundo* (*The World*) and *El Sol* (*The Sun*), to get competing views on the news. We also read *La Alarma* (a national rag featuring the most gruesome crimes in the country) as well as a slew of fashion magazines, which my *amá* Chencha copied to sew my stylish clothes, and movie magazines with the latest celebrity gossip. I would read with her, often asking questions and getting the background on everything I didn't understand. Around 4:30 we would get up and go downtown, either to the movies (I saw every *Ben Hur* movie ever made) or to have coffee and *pan dulce* (sweet bread) at a popular restaurant owned by a Chinese family in the middle of the Chinese section of Tampico. *El Mundo* (The World) Restaurant was the popular spot for people to enjoy the latest news by chatting with others, playing dominos, and people watching. If we went to the movies, my *amá* Chencha would pack *jamón* (ham) sandwiches with *pan frances* (French rolls) and *chiles en vinagre* (pickled hot peppers). We would also take along bottles of Pepsi and eat while we watched two movies in a row with a very short intermission for a quick restroom break.

This was my childhood—full of vibrancy, stimulation, education, caring, and love. I learned that life is supposed to be exciting and full of connection with all sorts of people. I was taught by people within and outside my family that the public sphere is not to be feared, rejected, or neglected. I was taught that we are citizens of the world and that knowledge is not only found in books but also in conversation, touch, taste, dialogue, and exploration. I was shown through example and direct communication that knowledge is to be respected and shared. I chose my profession because I thought that was life. I facilitate the path of others toward education because that is what many did for me. Ultimately, I learned that the public good is what makes us human and happy.

Hermana Número Dos: María Avon[3] Hurtado, aka Bonnie, Bonifacha, Facha,[4] Güera,[5] _____ Fill in the Blank

As I looked around the auditorium, there was not a dry eye, including my own. *Ya de por si soy bien chillona* (I tend to cry easily anyway), and I really let it all hang out that night. A Spanish-speaking mother was at the podium describing the transformation of her 21-year-old son during the past year. For the first time in 10 years, she could sleep peacefully at night, knowing her son was on the right path. After she sat down, a father stood up and spoke about his feelings of helplessness in keeping his 17-year-old son out of trouble. The father knew full well that his son was headed to prison or possible death by gang violence unless the family moved back to Mexico. These stories were told during the 2003 Clean Slate Tattoo Removal Graduation Ceremony in the city of San Jose, California. As the deputy director of the Parks, Recreation and Neighborhood Services Department, I was prepared to give a speech that night to thank the graduates for their commitment to stay in the program, the parents for their support of the graduates, and the many volunteer doctors who helped with removing the tattoos. By the standards of most publicly funded parks and recreation departments in this country, this program was not considered a traditional activity. In fact, the program was very controversial and faced budget cuts on a yearly basis. However, community support for the program was unwavering. My experience defending this program made me appreciate the advice given by several mentors over the years; they recommended that I seek positions of authority within government agencies and make decisions that make a difference in

---

[3] I was supposed to be given the middle name Yvonne after a kind French Canadian woman my mother met in *El Norte* when our family traveled from Texas to Michigan to pick crops. My mother did not know how to spell Yvonne, and the only name that came to mind was Avon (yes, as in Avon Products, which were sold in Mexico). Thus, my birth certificate officially states that my middle name is Avon, although my nickname "Bonnie" is based on the intended name of Yvonne.

[4] My Spanish-speaking relatives and friends found it difficult to relate to the name Bonnie, so my grandmother translated it to Bonifacia and then to Bonifacha, which is based on alliteration. However, this latter version seemed quite long for a young child, so the nickname was reduced to Facha.

[5] *Güera* is Spanish for "fair skinned." As I take after my maternal grandfather, who was also *güero* with hazel eyes, I was given yet another nickname.

the community. The most valuable lesson I learned in the course of my career is the importance of mobilizing community support to keep controversial, nontraditional initiatives alive. *Pero, está dura la cosa!* (But, it is not an easy task!) Why have I taken on this assignment of serving the public as my life's mission? I believe the answer lies in my upbringing.

My Roots

Unlike my older sister, Aída, I grew up primarily in McAllen, Texas—a true *Tejana* in soul, spirit, and heart. Even today, after living in beautiful Northern California for 15 years, *de vez en cuando, se me sale* (every now and then, I unconsciously switch to) *el Tejano* twang: *con, el* "really? *Apoco?*" (Really? You don't say?). Even my enlightened Californian sense of nutrition, health, and fitness does not prevent me from indulging at "Whataburger" or the locally owned "*El Pato*" or "*Cuevas*" when I visit *el valle* (the valley in south Texas, as the region is known). Beyond the great food, however, what tugs at my memory the most are the friendly, down-to-earth people of my childhood. In spite of the conservative valley politics and poverty-level conditions, my experiences in the valley have profoundly shaped my career path.

My journey toward a profession on behalf of the public good began, as it does for most, with my parents and my extended family. Everyone in my family is extremely hardworking and passionate about life. I vividly remember my parents' work ethic. It was not uncommon for me to be awakened at 11:00 p.m., when I heard my father's car in the driveway, arriving home from his 18-hour work day. With excitement, I would hop out of bed, make him a cup of coffee, and sit down at the kitchen table to catch up on our days' activities. This was my opportunity to have some time alone with him. I felt the same anticipation when my mother drove up late at night after her double shifts at the hospital in Reynosa. My parents' examples taught me much about hard work and perseverance.

My family members were not the only ones working hard and committing to the collective good. Our entire neighborhood consisted of many hardworking families that took care of each other. Growing up in the valley in a neighborhood that created community through conversation and social events, I was exposed to multiple surrogate parents. Many eyes were upon me, especially because my parents worked evenings. When my older sister left for graduate school at the University of Michigan and my brother left after high school graduation to join the Navy, my stand-in family in McAllen became *los vecinos* (the neighbors), who were very comfortable scolding me if I got into trouble and telling my parents about my mischievous behavior while they were at work.

El valle is a very conservative region where "virtue" (read virginity) is considered a prized possession. In fact, my mother was so concerned about my "virtue" that I was required to marry at 16 because I had stayed out late with my boyfriend. Once married, I dropped out of high school and worked full time to support us. The marriage to my homeboy/husband lasted less than a year. I got back on track and obtained my GED soon after my divorce. This began my pattern of being "on and off" my journey toward higher education. Obviously, I did not choose the easiest path to obtain an education, but it certainly was one that tests individual strength. Surviving the journey, as bumpy as it was for me, is in itself a testimony to what my parents taught me: "Stay in school; it's the only way to get ahead" was the family message that guided me through my 20s.

Until I was 26, I knew no other world except the valley. All of my values and attitudes about marriage, education, family, and poverty had been absorbed from living in this isolated area, situated along the U.S.-Mexican border and spawning extremely conservative politics, profound poverty, *y mucho corazón* (and a lot of heart). I always felt that my roots, including my hometown, contained both good and bad aspects. I consciously chose not to condemn them out of hand, but instead to embrace that which was good and reject that which was harmful. Of course, the process of deciphering which was which, as liberating as it was, also entailed many growing pains. Endless conversations, primarily with my older sister, helped me clarify my path and identify which aspects of my roots I wanted to retain and which I wanted to leave behind.

Political Awakenings

In addition to learning through conversations with my older sister, I observed injustices around me that began to make a difference in my thinking. As I described earlier, my father had an unwavering work ethic. He worked as a loader packing *repollo* (cabbage), *lechuga* (lettuce), and other vegetables for the Teddy Bertuca Warehouse, a locally owned packing company in McAllen. In the 18 years my father labored at the plant, under the worst conditions imaginable, he never missed a day of work. I vividly remember the day my father's supervisor called the house, annoyed that my father was absent from work. Despite my father's perfect attendance record, the supervisor never assumed that he might have a good reason for not showing up. The supervisor did not modify his irritated tone, even after learning that my father had suffered a fatal heart attack while he was visiting family in Tampico. During his entire tenure at the Teddy Bertuca Company, my father never received health insurance, retirement, or vacation benefits, and at the time of his death at age 59, he was paid minimum wage. This was one of many painful injustices I witnessed, wrongdoings that stoked a fire in my belly. I was determined to follow a career path that allowed me to work for people who faced these types of prejudices and lack of caring.

Personal Transformations/Geographical Dislocations

Four years after a second marriage and divorce and the birth of my daughter, Chanel (aka Chanelita,[6] Channel 2,[7] Homey,[8] _____ fill in the blank), I moved to California to live with my older sister, Chata. At this point, she was an assistant professor of psychology at the University of California in Santa Cruz. My daughter was barely four, and I was terrified to leave the only "home" I had ever known. I had reached the painful conclusion that I needed to leave the valley to create a better life for my daughter and myself. My younger sister, Arcelia, had moved to Berkeley three years earlier to start her undergraduate degree at the University of California, Berkeley. I was working as a secretary at Pan American University (the local college next to McAllen) in Edinburg, Texas. Through the encouragement of my direct supervisor, history professor Rodolfo Rocha, I had begun taking college courses part time. Unwittingly, I had earned enough credits and maintained a high enough grade point average that I was able to transfer from Pan American University to the University of California in Santa Cruz (UCSC).

Culture shock does not begin to describe what I experienced when I

---

[6] Our Spanish-speaking relatives could not easily pronounce the name, Chanel, so they began calling my daughter Chanelita (the nickname is based on alliteration, but it also means "little shoe"), which was particularly appropriate because Chanel was an unusually small baby.

[7] Chanel's *tio* Craig started calling her "Channel 2" after the local television news channel because Chanel, as a five-year-old, loved making the hand sign for that channel.

[8] During the early 1990s, there was a TV comedy show called *In Living Color*, one of the few television shows written and produced by African American writers. As a five-year-old, Chanel memorized many of the skits word for word, and her imitation of "Homey the Clown," whose signature saying was "Homey, don't play that!" was uncannily accurate.

arrived at Santa Cruz in 1991. In a UCSC sociology class, we discussed whether I was Chicana, Latina, Hispanic, Mexican American, and so on. Coming from the valley, where 98% of the residents are of Mexican descent, self-identity was a given and hardly ever a question, *era mexicana y ya!* (I was simply Mexican). At the time, I honestly could not understand the relevance of the question. The classes and professors I was exposed to nurtured my critical thinking skills, resulting in tremendous personal growth. However, I still felt very much out of place in Santa Cruz. The people were different. I had never seen White people with dreadlocks, and I could not find a taco stand anywhere, only tofu, which to this day I do not know what it is made of. As luck would have it, I discovered Watsonville, a rural agricultural community 15 miles south of Santa Cruz, where I felt right at home. I identified with the people's friendliness and, of course, the smells and tastes of Mexican food in the city's many restaurants. At the time I was enrolled in the master's program in social work at San Jose State University. I began my integration into the Watsonville community by volunteering for political campaigns and nonprofit organizations where I met many community-oriented people. I developed long-lasting relationships that nurtured me and helped me develop my commitment to the public good.

My motivation for pursuing a degree in social work was primarily to help the farm-working community. In this vein, I worked with a research company in charge of conducting a national farmworker survey for the U.S. Department of Labor. The purpose of the survey was to assess farm workers' wages, access to health care, and living conditions. I continued to work in the nonprofit sector when I became the executive director of Fenix Services, an alcohol- and drug-counseling agency. I met many courageous people through this work, not only the people we served in our programs, but the people who provided the services as well. I learned that people could be leaders regardless of their life circumstances. The common goal was to voice the needs and concerns of disenfranchised communities. I developed an incredible sense of responsibility and commitment to join the good fight. My motivation was fueled by the knowledge that if the cosmic gods had sneezed at the wrong moment, I, too, might have been a recipient of the services I was administering. I knew that I was one of the rare individuals who had the opportunity to obtain an education and the privilege to work in their chosen field.

The Role of Mentors

Currently I am director of the Parks and Community Services Department in the city of Tracy, California. When I reflect on my arrival in Santa Cruz, California, 15 years ago, with my daughter, as a single parent receiving food stamps and trying to get through college living with my sister in her two-bedroom apartment, I realize how many transformations I have experienced. I also acknowledge that I did not arrive where I am today without the help and support of many. Special people have guided me along the way, beginning with my older sister, who has provided consistent, pragmatic advice and guidance, keeping me focused during the times when I wandered "off track."

Other mentors surfaced outside of the family. Individuals like Dania Torres Wong, who worked with California Rural Legal Assistance and was one of the founders of *Poder Latino* (Latino Power), a volunteer group that sought to identify and mentor Latinos and Latinas for political office and employment in the public sector. Dania is currently personnel officer for the County of Santa Cruz, where she continues to recruit people who are committed to helping the community. Her quiet dedication, nonjudgmental demeanor, and unwavering loyalty provided a role model that resonated with me. She was the kind of person I wanted to become.

Another mentor and friend, Celia Organista, is one of the fieriest 60-year-olds I've ever met. She went as far as high school, did not start working outside the home until she was in her 40s, and had raised her family. Celia is a longtime resident of Watsonville, where she lives with her husband of 40 years in a mobile home on the land of a farm grower, her husband's employer. Celia is director of Women's Crisis Support (a nonprofit organization helping women who suffer domestic violence) and is one of the most influential political leaders in Santa Cruz County and beyond. She has no qualms about stomping up the steps of city hall or contacting politicians when her organization's needs are ignored. Celia has been in my life consistently since my move to California. Her personal commitment to making a difference in her community through politics, work, and relentless advocacy paved the way for other Latinos to run for City Council in Watsonville and influence policy changes that positively affect and serve women who experience domestic violence. Role models such as these are invaluable. They helped me define my path through their examples of engaging in the public good.

Reflections and Conclusions

In reviewing my life in this essay, I pinpoint the influences that allowed me to find the work that nurtures me as it nurtures others. I have concluded that the values of hard work and perseverance fortified me through the good, the bad, and the ugly, *como quien dice* (as one would say). These values, which I consider the pillars of my survival, were difficult to instill in my own daughter, Chanel. In seeing her grow up, I realized that it is not through conversation or experience alone that a young person internalizes values. These values have to become so natural to one's being that doing a good job and persevering in the face of adversity just "is." For me, it was the combination of what I learned at home, the experiences I had outside the home, the exposure to formal education, and the significant mentors who ultimately launched me into a career that has made seeking the public good second nature to me.

Hermanita Número Tres (Little Sister Number Three): Arcelia Leticia,[9] aka Arcy, Arcy Farcy, Arce,[10] *La Mano* (The Hand),[11] Chelita,[12] _____ Fill in the Blank.

More than anything else, parenthood has clarified for me why I pursued (and sometimes endured) higher education, and why I use my degrees for the public good. This past year I have played parent to my older sister's teenage daughter and have also become a parent to a son born just three weeks ago.

---

[9] My middle name, Leticia, was given to me by my sister, Bonnie, who was seven when I was born in the Mexican border town of Reynosa, Tamaulipas, across from McAllen. My mother had me by cesarean and was unable to leave the car when my father filled out the forms for my birth certificate at the government registry in Reynosa. Bonnie accompanied my father, and when the registrar asked for a middle name, Bonnie jumped up and shouted her favorite name, "Leticia!" My father simply agreed; my mother was shocked when she read the birth certificate years later because she had no idea where the name Leticia had come from.

[10] The first point of departure for renaming all of us (as I'm sure is the case in other Spanish-speaking families) is alliteration. If it sounds funny, beautiful, melodic, your name is changed appropriately—that is the origin of Arcy Farcy. My sister Chata was in high school when I was born. She was reading Chaucer when she discovered that *arse* meant ass, so she thought it would be funny to call me Arce.

[11] Our family was so eccentric that we jokingly referred to ourselves as the *mexicano* version of *The Addams Family*, the popular television show in the 1970s. The Addams family's living room was equipped with a box that contained a hand that popped out to answer the phone, dust, and do other chores. I was the youngest in my family, and as such, whenever anyone in my family wanted something, they would send me to get it—thus the moniker, "*La Mano*."

[12] My father gave me this name when I was a newborn. Chelita is diminutive for Arcelia.

In attempting to guide my niece, I was forced to articulate for another (alarmingly suggestible) human being, my purpose in life. *Uy cucuy!* (Scary!) The conversation went like this:

> Me: So, have you thought about what you want to do with your life?
>
> My niece: I don't know . . .
>
> Me: (maybe a tad impatiently, OK . . . a lot impatiently) What do you mean, you don't know! Well, don't you want to *help people*? Do things for others? Or do you just want to eat, sleep, and perform bodily functions? (I might have used different terminology.)

(*nb:* This is normally an effective method of questioning, which I learned in law school, because it forces the person being cross-examined to give the only answer any decent human being could possibly give under the circumstances.)

> My niece: Yes, of course I do! (You see? Mission accomplished!)

After this highly useless conversation, I realized the futility of ordering someone to have a purpose in life. To be effective, individuals have to embrace their purpose so that it becomes part of their core being. My main concern in deciding to become a parent was not how I would pay for my son's education (not to mention his diapers), but how I would infuse my son with the same purpose that I was given by my family and mentors. What if I failed in giving him a purpose? I would fail myself, my family, but, most important, my community.

Naming and Hoping

After much deliberation, I named my son Joaquin after the epic poem, "I Am Joaquin," by Rodolfo "Corky" Gonzales (1969), which became the anthem for the Chicano civil rights movement of the 1960s. The beautiful poem reads:

> I am Joaquin.
>> I must fight
>>> And win this struggle
>>> for my sons, and they

must know from me
Who I am. . . .
The part of blood that is mine
has labored endlessly five-hundred
years under the heel of lustful
Europeans
I am still here!
I have endured in the rugged mountains
of our country
I have survived the toils and slavery
of the fields.
I have existed
in the barrios of the city,
in the suburbs of bigotry,
in the mines of social snobbery,
in the prisons of dejection,
in the muck of exploitation
and
in the fierce heat of racial hatred.

And now the trumpet sounds,
The music of the people stirs the
Revolution,
Like a sleeping giant it slowly
rears its head
to the sound of
Tramping feet
Clamoring voices
Mariachi strains
Fiery tequila explosions
The smell of chile verde and
Soft brown eyes of expectation for a
better life.
And in all the fertile farm lands,
the barren plains,
the mountain villages,
smoke smeared cities
We start to MOVE.
La Raza!

Mejicano!
Español!
Latino!
Hispano!
Chicano!
or whatever I call myself,
I look the same
I feel the same
I cry
and
Sing the same
I am the masses of my people and
I refuse to be absorbed.
I am Joaquin
The odds are great
but my spirit is strong
My faith unbreakable
My blood is pure
I am Aztec Prince and Christian Christ
I SHALL ENDURE!
I WILL ENDURE!

I thought my son's name would be a constant reminder (if not a hammer beating him over the head) of his roots and his purpose in life: to care about the common good as much as he cares about his own. I hope that when he is old enough to read the poem he will feel the same sense of pride that my father taught me to have as a *mexicana* in a country that does not honor its immigrant heritage.

My son's middle name is Guadalupe, after my father, the person who was the single most positive force in my life, only to be replaced by my oldest sister after he passed away when I was in high school. My father was not formally educated, but he taught me everything I know about humane values and caring for other people. He always told me to be proud of myself and showed me through example. Learning to read and write in Spanish, our national language, was one way to keep me proud of my heritage. I remember spending Sundays with my father (his only day off from his grueling farmwork), driving across the border to Reynosa, Mexico, where we would buy dozens of comic books (for me), newspapers, and even *La Alarma*, a

National Inquirer-type rag (which apparently is a family tradition, since my oldest sister read them with my grandmother, too, as a child). We then proceeded to the plaza to buy a *licuado de platano* (banana milkshake) and sit on a bench to enjoy the sun as people strolled by. Afterward we would head back to our home on the other side of the border. At home, we parked ourselves in the living room—my father on the couch, me at his feet on the floor—to read the rest of the day and watch whatever soccer game happened to be on television. Our Sunday ritual never varied. By the time I was six years old and started kindergarten in McAllen, Texas, I had become a fluent reader and was so verbally articulate (in Spanish, of course) that my lovely siblings took to tape-recording me in conversation so they could laugh at me later. They also nicknamed me *la enana* (midget), more out of disrespect for me than anything else, because I was small in stature but tall in verbal skills.

Disruptions and Growth

My protected home environment of love and comfort was disrupted when I entered kindergarten before bilingual education was available in the public schools. My language skills in Spanish did not buffer me from the shock I suffered when I entered the classroom. I could not understand a single word anyone was saying, an extremely traumatizing experience that I can still remember in detail to this day. Fortunately, I quickly learned English and excelled academically throughout middle and high school. My parents' constant encouragement expressed in countless ways ensured my survival in school. I overcame many educational obstacles and ended up at the University of California, Berkeley, as an undergraduate majoring in political science and Chicano studies.

My professors at Berkeley became my surrogate parents; they gave birth to me intellectually and politically. My professors taught me that family is not about blood, but about a common commitment to the same values, in our case, about making our community a priority in our lives and our work. Among the professors who influenced me was Dr. Julia Curry Rodriguez; she showed me that I indeed belonged at UC Berkeley and that I had the ability to succeed. Dr. Larry Trujillo taught me that school is not just about memorizing facts, regurgitating them within the confines of a blue book, and earning good grades, content in the knowledge that I would one day make a good living. Rather, Dr. Trujillo encouraged his students to use their intellectual capacities for the public good. Largely through his encouragement, I designed a program with my fellow undergraduate classmates to teach English as a second language to Spanish-speaking Latino inmates at San Quentin State Prison. I am proud to report that the program is still running at UC Berkeley after 17 years. We religiously (in the truest sense of the word) rented a van and drove 50 miles to San Quentin every week so that we could visit and instruct Latino inmates, many of whom did not speak a word of English. Many of these inmates had been sentenced to prison for an unreasonable number of years for mostly nonviolent, drug-related crimes. Rather than hardened criminals, they were mostly young people in need of medical attention for drug addiction. In many instances, they had not encountered anyone in the criminal justice system, including their attorneys, who spoke their language (literally or figuratively) and could advocate effectively for them. Through these visits to prison, I came to see the inmates as part of my community.

Aligning oneself with inmates is not inconsequential in this society, which does not believe in the redemption of individuals who commit crimes and are incarcerated. The person who taught me to be proud of serving this most marginalized segment of the country's society was my surrogate father, Dr. Craig Haney, my oldest sister's husband. Craig continued my moral and social education after my father died. Uncannily, Craig stood for many of the same things that my father stood for: compassion, courage, loyalty, and an uncompromising work ethic. Watching Craig represent people on death row in a caring and committed way inspired me to emulate his dedication. Armed with the values I saw and admired in Craig, I had no choice but to study law and become a public defender.

The Injustice of the Justice System

Law school, as well as the legal profession, was not designed for people like me. The apparent rationality of the law disguises the raw power it has to act in purely punitive ways on those who have the least amount of power—the poor, the uneducated, and people of color. Anyone who challenges the allocation of the law's irrationality is not welcome in the legal profession. I survive as a public defender by reminding myself of my roots and my purpose in life. Because of who I am and how I was raised, I cannot practice law in mainstream ways. In the most basic meaning of public defender, I defend the public. I talk to people who have been condemned to death by the state and present their stories in ways that I hope will make decision makers see a bit of themselves in the inmates' life trajectories. My current work is an extension of what I did when I taught English at San Quentin; I try to see the humanity and individual in all inmates. They are part of my community, not separate from where I come from. Granted, it is not an easy task. My profession does not value the work I do, nor does mainstream society. But I know that my family is behind me. They understand that I have no other choice (especially if I want to have a chair at the family dinner table!). I work for the public good because I must. There is nothing I would rather do; I owe it to my family, my community, myself, but, most importantly, my clients. I work for the public good because of all these interlocking forces, in the knowledge that I have a debt to be repaid that is so large and that is owed to so many people that the only way that I can repay it is by living and breathing work that benefits the public good. Equally important, I have a commitment to teaching my child to do the same.

My deepest wish is that one day, when my son is old enough to understand, he, too, will find inspiration in the same poem that made my skin ripple with pride as a first-year student, wide-eyed and curious, at UC Berkeley. There I sat because my older sister forced me to, my father would have wanted me to, and my mother bravely allowed me to. Chicano studies professors at that institution taught me about myself, my history and community, and what my purpose in life should be: to give back to my community everything I had been fortunate enough to receive. "The more you know, the more you owe": this message was communicated loudly and clearly. It is a message I try to honor every day and one that I hope to pass on to those around me.

Conclusion

Each sister's narrative begins with a list of names given to us by our families and extended communities. As illustrated in the rest of the chapters in this book, bestowing nicknames is not an uncommon practice within Mexicano/ Latino communities. Naming and renaming one another illustrates the fluidity of familial relationships and the weaving in and out of different identities, depending on who is doing the "naming." All three of us have multiple monikers that call up different relationships and experiences that have made us who we are. For example, no one in the family or extended family uses "Aída," because it suggests a formality and distance that seem awkward and inappropriate. On the other hand, should someone not close with Aída address her as "Chata," that would be regarded as highly insulting. Likewise, only a few people call Arcelia "Chelita," because it was our father, who passed away when she was 16, who gave her that term of endearment.

We believe that our multiple names gave us the ability to know various aspects of ourselves, which, in turn, facilitated the recognition of multiple strengths. In our youth, we were not one-dimensional people with fixed dispositions and limited talents, but complex human beings who existed in relation to significant others in our environment. Each name, nickname, moniker calls forth different facets of ourselves and, with it, the memory of oneself as having multiple talents and as belonging to different communities.

We have taken this knowledge of self into our respective professions. When we need the strength to continue our struggles, we draw from each other, by simply making a call, sending an e-mail, and, most recently, posting a text message: "Hey, Bonns, want to have dinner on Sunday? Call Arce the Farce and see if she can make it." No matter how difficult our day has been, we are pulled back to our roots, our community, our sense of mission, and our purpose. From this, we gather ourselves to continue the good fight for the public good.

References

Cervantes, L. D. (1988). Visions of Mexico while at a writing symposium in Port Townsend, Washington. In Richard Elleman and Robert O'Clair (Eds.), *The Norton Anthology of Modern American Poetry* (2nd ed.) (pp. 1729–1731). New York: W. W. Norton.

Cisneros, S. (2002). *Caramelo*. New York: Alfred A. Knopf.

Esquivel, L. (1992). *Like Water for Chocolate*. New York: Doubleday.

Gonzales, R. C. (1969). *Yo soy Joaquin*. Unpublished manuscript.

MIGUEL GUAJARDO

FRANCISCO GUAJARDO

5

TWO BROTHERS IN
HIGHER EDUCATION

Weaving a Social Fabric for Service in Academia

Miguel Guajardo and Francisco Guajardo

S ince we were young children, we recall family stories about working
toward the public good. Our father tells stories of his mother, our
Abuela Virginia, who managed the affairs of the modest family ranch,
el rancho Alameda, in the Municipio Dr. Cos in the northern Mexican state
of Nuevo Leon. Virginia saw a steady stream of wandering *mexicanos* between the 1920s and the early 1950s trek from the interior of Mexico on their
way to the United States. *Mamá les daba de comer a todos que pasaban por el
rancho* (My mother fed everyone who walked through our ranch), recalls our
father, José Angel, as he describes how his mother practiced her own brand
of philanthropy. Our mother tells similar stories of how her mother, Agueda,
monitored the northward activity of immigrants who headed north of the
Rio Grande River, *y les daba refugio* (and she gave them refuge). *Abuela*
Agueda did this from her residence at Capote Ranch, which sits on the
northern bank of the river in Hidalgo County.

As working-class matriarchs living along the border during the first half
of the 20th century, our grandmothers had a particular appreciation for the
plight of working Mexicans who came across the border in search of a better
life, but they also seemed to raise children who understood the importance
of knowing those stories. They taught their children about a particular social
fabric for service as they wove the experiences through their stories (Villenas & Moreno, 2001). Our parents say they learned the stories through the

pláticas they heard from their parents, and as they transmitted the family stories to us through this distinct *plática* method, our epistemological condition was shaped; the *pláticas* informed the method through which we learned and knew the nature of our reality. The ontological dimensions, or the nature and form through which we made sense of our realities, were similarly encapsulated by *las pláticas* (Pizarro, 2001). This is a critical point for us as sons, brothers, fathers, teachers, researchers, and agents for community change. Every part of our work is driven by the stories we have learned, the stories we create, and the stories we imagine. We nurture and transmit stories to our families, our students, and to the public at large through *pláticas*, just as our *abuelas* and our parents did with us.

Stories have enriched the life of the family. To be sure, formal education has not been in great supply in the history of the family narrative; our grandparents spent just a tiny fraction of their time in a traditional school environment; our mother never attended school, though she recalls a traveling teacher making infrequent stops in the ranch where she was raised; and our father went up to the fourth grade, because that's as much education as *la*

Miguel, Francisco, Luis, and Juan Guajardo

escuela rural offered. Much like scores of other Mexican immigrant families, ours is similarly working-class, rural, and with limited experience in formal schools. Nevertheless, our father has penned his autobiography, and our mother has authored a decade-long oral history. When family *pláticas* focus on formal schooling, our father claims to have attended the most learned of all educational institutions, *La Universidad de la Vida* (the University of Life), as he calls it. Our family encyclopedia looks like a veritable compendium of oral stories, written documents, a series of videos, and a range of other visual representations. We learned through the stories as they have been manifested through words, images, pages and more recently digital media; we bring these experiences to our work as college professors.

When we arrived in this country as young children, our family's transnational road had already been paved. Our paternal grandfather, Silverio Alanís, traveled to Mesilla, New Mexico, during the 1880s to shear sheep. In his unpublished autobiography, our father writes about his own days as a young sheepherder in Nuevo Leon as an experience that simply built upon his own father's ranching tradition (Guajardo, 1986). When our mother, Julia, was born in 1934 in Mexico, she was born as a U.S. citizen. We were curious about this as young children and later found through collecting family oral histories that our mother's family fled El Capote Ranch on the U.S. side of the Texas-Mexican border in the late 1920s, as they eluded Texas Rangers who were searching for our grandfather. Our grandfather was purportedly a *bulega* (bootlegger) who, after committing a crime, gathered his wife, Agueda, and two young children and took them to Mexico, where they would be safe from the infamous *Rinches* who pursued him. Our mother would be born in the family's new home in Mexico just a few years later.

Growing up in a rural community and attending a public school system along the border, we were engulfed by waves of stories on a daily basis. When we attended Edcouch-Elsa High School in the early 1980s, the school district held the dubious distinction of being the poorest public school district in Texas, according to property tax base measures. The culture of the school, however, was anything but impoverished. Whereas objectified indicators suggested that high poverty rates, high unemployment, and low levels of adult educational attainment defined an impoverished school and community setting, local people did not seem to entirely heed those indicators. A robust spirit and culture permeated daily life (Kretzmann & McKnight, 1993). Locals embraced a community narrative that celebrated young people and their achievements, just as they respected the resiliency and struggles of the town's elders. In this context, the schools and community failed to use any clear vision or framework through which to develop the richness and vitality of its residents.

Our work as local educators has focused on building that framework: one based on identifying local assets and subsequently working to develop them. But this work is riddled with institutional complexities. Opportunities for this work abound in the schools, but the bureaucratic and impersonal nature of the educational institutions within which we have worked during the past 15 years also have created numerous obstacles to community-building initiatives. On one hand, the public high school out of which we have worked has allowed space to engage in community-based research work, youth leadership initiatives, and sundry other developmental work. The universities we work in today similarly offer spaces for creativity and innovation. On the other hand, both places are driven by sets of standards that have little to do with the life, spirit, or pulse of the community outside the educational institutions. The standards and testing mania that govern school cultures in the early part of the 21st century come increasingly closer to suffocating the creative impulses of teachers in the public schools and professors in universities (McNeil, 2000; Valenzuela, 2005). Our experience as public school teachers and university professors has taught us the necessity of exploring different avenues, sometimes outside the institution, to engage in work that matters to us and matters to the community. In this context, we founded a nonprofit educational organization in 1997, the Llano Grande Center for Research and Development, with offices at a local high school (the Center also owns a retreat house in the rural countryside) but which operates independently of the control of the public school and the universities out of which we teach and work.

First Person Commentary—Francisco

After completing a bachelor's and a master's degree from the University of Texas at Austin, I returned to teach at our alma mater, Edcouch-Elsa High School (E-E HS), while Miguel stayed in Austin learning the trade of organizing youth, parents, and community members for the purpose of creating greater educational opportunities for Latino and African American students in East Austin. During the early 1990s, I initiated a college placement program that quickly gained regional and, eventually, national attention. From one of the most impoverished high schools in the state, dozens of Mexican American students began to gain entrance into some of the most exclusive universities in the country, most of them Ivy League schools. By the mid-1990s, however, I had worked with other teachers and with Miguel to modify this work by infusing a significant community-based research focus into the college placement work. That's when Miguel and I founded the Llano Grande Center as a research enterprise focused on training students to conduct oral histories, organize asset mapping and development exercises, and institute local social change initiatives grounded in a different pedagogy (Freire, 1970).

The work of the Llano Grande Center is consistent with our work as college professors. The range of programming hosted by the Center includes teacher training, youth community leadership, digital storytelling, economic development, and capturing both personal and community narratives. At the university, we participate in developing emerging public school leaders who undergo reflexive exercises in personal and community understandings. Through the Center and the university, we use the *plática* methods we learned from our parents, grandparents, *tíos* and *tías*, and others in the community that raised us. We teach through *plática*, as much as we teach through story and the narrative form.

In the following text, we present an overview of the work in which we have been engaged for the past 15 years. This conceptual framework (see Figure 5.1) provides an overview and an outline that frames the work.

Building Networks of Service

Method

Consistent with the ontological position of our personal development, we use the method most theoretically consistent and epistemologically congruent with our educational development. This method disrupts the traditional order of things; it precedes the traditional research question and identification of the problem statement. The *plática,* or dialogue (Bohm, 1996), is the activity we engaged in during afternoons with our parents as we sat around the kitchen table, or as we sat on the porch and ate watermelon to assuage

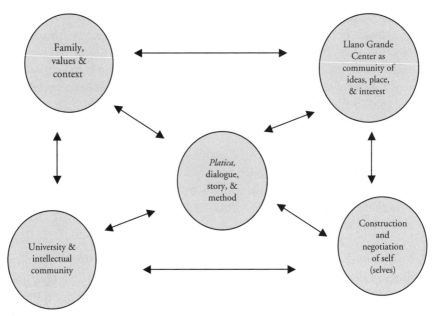

FIGURE 5.1
A SOCIAL AND POLITICAL NETWORK

the oppressive South Texas heat. We learned at a young age that the *plática* was an act of sharing ideas, experiences, and stories. This process was reciprocal as our parents gave us an opportunity to pose questions or just provide the platform to exercise their skills. We recall our older brother, Pepe, using the *plática* space to imitate the play-by-play announcers of the Bravos de Reynosa, the regional team from the Liga Mexicana. He began by announcing the starting lineup, transformed himself into a batter, then became baserunner as he sped around the neighborhood in an attempt to beat out the shortstop's throw to first base. The *pláticas* created the stage for the game of life. Everybody had an opportunity to display skills; this display was not about schooling, however; it was about teaching, learning and sharing. This was also the place where our parents read to us.

The *plática* (Padilla, 1993) created the knowledge and allowed for the multiple realities to be (re)presented without being ridiculed. There was great laughter, but there was even more admiration for everyone's willingness to participate in the *plactica,* and even more in the collective growth. It made sense that when we grew up and became teachers and researchers we would use this same strategy to teach and learn. The *plática* as method is authentic and has an inherent robust quality. When we were growing up, we understood never to violate the chief ingredient of the *plática—la palabra* (the word). The *plática* pushes the researchers' comfort zone, for without authenticity, the *plática* will not yield the necessary currency needed for building community and conducting sound research. The *plática* requires the facilitator to become open and vulnerable, as the *plática* process becomes reciprocal. The *plática* also has been a valuable tool in our community work, particularly as a mechanism through which we share information, build relationships, and collect data. It can be used in a one-on-one conversation, a house meeting (small, purposeful group gathering), focus group, classroom conversation, and/or as a community-organizing tool.

Additional data sources used to inform this chapter include personal, family, and community reflections, stories, over 15 years of community work experience, and the archives of the Llano Grande Center for Research and Development. The Center has been the principle vehicle for the public work we identify in this document, but it is expanded to make sense of the impact this work has had personally and professionally.

As reflected in the framework, the method is critically important, because it is the *plática* that informs and filters the stories coming from each of the quadrants in the model. We make sense of the work through this anchor of *plática* and the world that we have collectively constructed.

The research questions guiding this document include:

- What informs our commitment to the common good?
- What are the structures and process that nurture activism and work toward the common good?
- What is the impact of this work on the self, the community, and the institutions of higher education?
- Why is the *plática* a vehicle for public engagement?
- What problems, or obstacles, have we encountered in the academy?

Contributions and Impact

Family, Values, and Context

The pedagogy of family and story informs our view of the public good. As our parents shared the stories of our *abuelitas* in our own home and in our community, we saw the daily acts of human kindness, which were always unconditional. One particular event reminds us of this thematic, when our father, Papi, taught us an important lesson in the public good.

One afternoon in the early 1980s, we rode with our father down Highway 107 heading west toward Edinburg, Texas, in our red and white 1974 Ford pickup truck. We recall the years because it was during the time of great political unrest in Central America. Living along the border, we saw many people pass through; many were men fleeing the military. Others were whole families leaving their country because of their political positions. Most of these people had few options; they had to leave or face death—this was the common story.

On this day, as we drove west, we saw a young man and an older gentleman running across the highway. They had the same look of exhaustion and fear we had become accustomed to seeing on others who had come before them. Our father stopped the vehicle and drove in reverse on the shoulder of the road. He stuck his head out of the truck and called the strangers to come over. Our father stepped out of the truck first, followed by us, and he began a conversation with them. The conversation seemed natural, nonthreatening; it even seemed like one that they had been engaged in for years. After about 20 minutes of talking, our father put his hand in his pocket and pulled out some cash. He reached out and gave the money to the older gentleman. He ended the conversation with the traditional *buenas suerte y que les vaya bien* (good luck and have a safe trip).

We got back into the truck. As adolescents we had all kinds of things going on in our minds, ranging from imagining the fear the boy was experiencing to why our father gave them money. To be sure, our father never gave us any cash. With his customary vision, our father saw through us, or maybe he just felt that this was the right time to share a story. He began by sharing that when he saw the men in the rearview mirror, he had to stop because he saw himself. As a young man growing up in Mexico, he and his brothers repeatedly crossed the Rio Grande to search for work in the agricultural fields in the United States. He was what is frequently referred to as a *mojado* (wetback or undocumented worker). For a number of years as a teenager he crossed the river, worked, and then headed back home on the weekends. On this day, he saw himself in the young man. He simultaneously saw himself in the older man as he saw his own children in the younger man. In a matter of seconds, all of these memories, emotions, and visions crossed his mind.

The connections he made are what allowed him to engage in conversation with the stranger as if it were an ongoing one. Our father and these men had been in the same situation at different points in history, yet in their minds, they were occupying the same space and shared similar experiences. This was very powerful, but the most important lesson was yet to come.

We did not mention the money; we just never talked about money in our house. Money was an adult issue, and our parents were responsible for this until we began to work ourselves. But again, he saw right through us and asked, "*¿Saben porque les dí dinero?*" (Do you know why I gave them money?)

The obvious answer would be *sí*, "yes we know why you gave them money," though we also thought about how he never gave us any money. We respected our father too much, however, to question his motives. Nonetheless, he knew that there was more to our response, so he reminded us of his own experiences as a young man crossing the border to help his family. He reminded us of our own migrant farmworking experiences and the difficulties we had while on the road and away from home. Then he began to share a story our grandmother had frequently told him.

We only knew our grandmother from his stories; she died when our father was a teenager. From his stories we could always tell the love our father had for his mother, and the stories still grip us in an emotionally powerful way. Living in rural Mexico, where there was no medical care, *Abuelita* Virginia died in our father's arms. Our father shared with us that her *consejos* taught him how to become a responsible man. And it seemed appropriate for him to share a *dicho* that he frequently heard from our *abuelita*: "*Ayer fuí yo, hoy son ellos, pero mañana serán mis hijos!*" (Yesterday it was me, today it's them, and tomorrow it will be my children . . . who need the help [see Waite, Nelson, & Guajardo, 2006]).

After sharing this *dicho*, he did not need to say any more. We knew exactly what his message meant. The cycle of life was placed before our eyes within a social justice construct. We knew that the deed our father had done was one of payback and pay forward, all in one. It was one of humanity within a reciprocal context. He had learned from his mother that he had benefited from the good deeds of others, and he had to pay back because his sons would be the beneficiaries of others' generosity in the future. We have not forgotten this lesson; it is part of what fuels our drive for justice and action; indeed, our children will be the beneficiaries of this work.

Construction and Negotiation of Self (Selves)

Our parents have always been very proud of who they are as human beings, but they are especially proud of who they are as political and spiritual beings. We always had a good dose of balance in our house. One parent would tend to act based on *que sea lo que dios quiera*, while the other was a bit more aggressive about the reality of the world and would say, *dios no cumple antojos*. So our reality was informed by this combination, which moved us to prayer at times, but mostly to action. Along with the *dios no cumple antojos*, there was that other issue of agency. As living beings we can create our own church wherever we were. Our father, mostly for convenience, quotes scripture. He says, "Wherever there are two or more in my name, there is a church." Though his statement always gave us an out for not showing up at church on Sunday, there are other lessons to be gleaned from those words. Inherent in his comment is that we have agency, and we have power to help *Dios* (God) make things happen. With God on your side, how can you go wrong? But it also raised the role of personal and collective responsibility for making things happen in our lives, our community, and—now—in higher education.

As undergraduate students who had graduated high school in one of the most economically depressed areas in the state and the poorest school district in the state of Texas, we did not have all of the academic tools to survive in the state flagship university.

First Person Commentary—Miguel

I was so out of the mainstream educational story that my higher education story begins at the local technical institution in South Texas; my first degree was in carpentry. In carpentry school, I figured out that knowledge and age were not congruent. But carpentry school was a fascinating experience because I was in a classroom with 30-, 40-, and 50-year-old men trying to find a career. They were attending school on the old Job Training Partnership Act resource. I always found it interesting that these older men would look for leadership and direction from someone like me, a 19-year-old student. While I was there, I also realized I needed to continue studying.

First Person Commentary—Francisco

While Miguel studied carpentry, I was finishing high school and thereafter enrolled as a freshman in one of the country's largest universities, the University of Texas at Austin. My freshman year was disastrous; my roommates and I lived about 15 miles from the university, I worked 30 hours per week as a cook at Kentucky Fried Chicken, I took a full course load, and tried to figure out how financial aid worked.

First Person—Miguel

I knew I had to continue to work; after all, our oldest brother, Pepe, had gone to the local college and laid the foundation, and our parents always expected us to do the same, though we were all trying to figure out what that meant. The first few years after high school were critical. For example, I basically learned how to read and write between the ages of 19 and 21; I never wrote a research paper or even an essay in high school. Fortunately, Pepe had just earned an English degree and teacher certification from the local college and was still living at home. At that time, Pepe taught me how to put words together to form sentences, sentences together to form paragraphs, and ideas together to write narratives.

First Person—Francisco

When I left for college, I immediately realized that I needed a strong support group to do well. As I struggled through my freshman year, I worked hard to convince Miguel to join me in Austin, after he completed carpentry school. As soon as Miguel finished his program, he applied for admission to the University of Texas at Austin, but he was rejected because of low ACT and SAT scores. After several semesters at Austin Community College, Miguel finally joined me at UT. Since that time, he and I have lived together and/or done our professional work together. All of this has been natural for my brother and me because we grew up in the same home, shared the same room, and simply grew up as close brothers.

We have constructed ourselves in the same image, spirit, and cultural practices as our parents. Though the surroundings and institutions have changed, our cultural being and identity have remained the same. Our political selves have been influenced by a radically different reality that has included rich academic and professional experiences that were not always positive or innocent. In fact, many of the direct messages countered the common and public good. It took much moral fiber and mutual support not to give in to the perverted power ideology of the institution and the soldiers who were training us. One of our saving graces was a handful of faculty who marched to a different beat. They recognized our work in the public sector and supported it. These supporters have become friends of our work and mentors in a number of areas.

These experiences have informed our development as human beings: our mother's compassion, our father's need for action and personal agency, our bothers' commitment to each other's well-being, and the academic training we have received from the institutions of the Western world that have created us as political beings. The actions of our political reality have been grounded by our need to recreate the *Universidad de la Vida* that our parents talk about and are so proud of belonging to. Our work for the public good is framed by this commitment to life, to community, and to each other. Our political selves have added the critical race elements that are central to the survival of a functional democracy. If democracy is to prevail, we must deal with the difficult issues of race, class, gender, and equity. To use this proposition is not an esoteric theoretical question; it is about engaging in true *pláticas*, research, and giving voice and legs to the ideas that surface from these *pláticas*. The strategies have changed, but the place and space have been constant. The next section articulates some of the public work in which we have engaged with our partners, but, to be sure, this would not have happened without our own development and growth as individuals, family members, and public intellectuals.

University and Intellectual Community

University faculty positions can be challenging environments in which to live and negotiate. There is a professorial culture that calls for particular behaviors and a certain kind of production. Though the position comes with a level of privilege, it also removes people from community-grounding work such as what we were engaged in throughout the 1980s and 1990s. The demands of being on campus, preparing for courses, holding office hours, publishing, and service work, which tends to be defined by how many committees one serves on, creates circumstances that preempt faculty members from maintaining close connections to work outside the university—that is, work in the community. The university culture becomes a dogma, and those who buy into the dogma may have a better opportunity to succeed, while those who resist are challenged to succeed. But what happens to those who survive the induction and continue to work within the institution? What does one keep, what does one give up, what does one sacrifice, and how does one adjust in order to contribute to the public good?

We do not spend much time debating other people's struggles in this document, but we do discuss what helped us survive the institutions we attended and how we have negotiated our own survival within the institutions in which we now work. The graduate program we attended was so technical that at different times, it pushed us out.

First Person Commentary—Francisco

I left graduate school for 12 years before coming back to complete a Ph.D. In the interim, I taught high school, engaged with youth in community-based research initiatives, and raised my family. Just as important, I came to realize, along with my brother, Miguel, the importance of creating our own institutions.

During those times, we both were engaged in community work; and as we did that, we also came to understand the necessity of establishing our own organization as a vehicle through which to practice higher education. In this context, we define higher education as social and cognitive construct, rather than linear, traditional construct. Because we view higher education as nonlinear, we function with the idea that youth do not need to wait until they are 18 years old and out of high school to engage in higher education; to the contrary, people can engage in higher education before they turn 18, and even if they are not enrolled in a higher education institution.

We founded the Llano Grande Center because of a need to put this notion into practice. And as we founded the organization, we saw our roles grow as public intellectuals who could operate with ideas and knowledge that were emerging from community, rather than from traditionally defined higher education institutions. The stories and other data emerging from the community also seemed to be at the cutting edge, where youth and adults working through research initiatives organized by the Llano Grande Center argued for a re-definition of knowledge, of higher education, of history, of

Left to right, Francisco and Miguel Guajardo

power. As the community voices pushed particular research and other agendas, we came to appreciate the slow speed of the traditional academic environment, where ideas cultivated therein tend to take shape three to five years after those same ideas are birthed and developed in the community. By the time traditional scholars collect data and write about and publish them, work in the community has moved beyond the literature. This is why it is essential to connect community practice to the literature and the theory, and vice versa. We must be conscious of the lag in time, but, more important, the research actions need to be relevant.

The relevance to the community work we do at the Llano Grande Center and the issues we deal with attracted the attention of some of our university faculty members. As we used the classes to write up our work, our mentors created the space for us to contribute to the academic world. This is when the academic growth began to take place; it was when we sat with faculty members and explored the intricacies of an issue, the practice, theory, and documentation that we began to get into the heads of our mentors. The publishing took place, but, most important, our relationships grew, and we began to craft a space for belonging at the university. When we engaged in *pláticas* with our mentors, we found that our work was important in the academy; it had its place in the literature, and it was possible to occupy the space in a university. Though we get our mail and we do our service to feed the institution, our work, research agenda, and service are primarily informed by the lessons our parents taught us and by the needs and energy that our community partners provide for us.

Though we are junior faculty, we come to this work with the reality that is not commonly seen or experienced at the university. We know that when we ask our colleagues to join us in a semester-long conversation with our local community, not too many are willing. But for those who are, we must be ready not only to propose the idea, but also to be willing to articulate the framework, the structure to implement the idea, and the framework for analysis. The *plática*, which seems organic to us, is not always the preferred pedagogical or research style to more mainstream academicians.

Our classrooms also challenge those students who are accustomed to simply listening to a lecture. They usually have to adjust to engaging in dialogue, which is typically about theory and practice. In our view, the role of the university is to engage with community and community issues at all levels, and our teaching is directly connected with the community. Our students are required to do community work through their assignments, service, or research, and our assignments are purposefully structured to affect the public good. The assignments range from tutoring and collecting oral histories or community stories to administering research and evaluation services for local programs and/or schools. Universities have a role in the development of communities, and we see ourselves as agents for facilitating this process and the community change that comes as a result of this work.

Problems

One of our most important mentors in the academy was Henry Trueba, who succumbed to cancer in the summer of 2004. As my brother and I stood by his deathbed early that summer, Henry looked at the two of us and firmly offered critical words of wisdom on two issues that we follow professionally and personally. First, he spoke about the importance of working together. "Whatever you do," he said, "make sure you stick together, because the academy is a very isolating place, and it can eat you up. Always work together, draw strength from each other."

After a lifetime of negotiating spaces of power in numerous academic posts across the country, Henry had particular insight regarding isolation in the academy. He shared stories of Latino junior faculty members who, in the absence of a strong support system, tended to drift to the margins of university life and, as a result, found it difficult to gain tenure. We have seen in our trek as junior faculty the product of both strong and weak support systems; but without question, the most important support has been that which we provide each other. While our departments on occasion have offered research, publishing, service, and other development opportunities, the most sustaining support is the one rooted in the lifelong relationships we have as brothers. Growing up in the same home, sharing the same room, sleeping on the same bed as children tends to help form strong bonds, and our experience is no exception. To be sure, we also draw strength from our community partners, with whom we have nurtured long-standing personal and professional relationships. Without those sustained relationships, however, the academy could very well, as Henry warned, "eat you up."

Second, Henry spoke about the importance of being faithful to the research agenda we had developed. Because our research is primarily rooted in the realities of South Texas youth, families, communities, and institutions, Henry understood the potential conflict between the type of research the university traditionally requires and the research with which we were already engaged.

"A focus on collecting voices of elders, children, and others, and using that as data," he once told us, "is legitimate as a research enterprise, but you may need to convince others in your academic departments that it is legitimate."

The problem with our research agenda has not necessarily been with our departments or colleagues; in fact, they have been very supportive. A greater source of tension has been what Padilla (2005) calls the formidable "culture of measurement" that has gripped public schools across the country. A critical part of our agenda focuses on finding and cultivating stories in schools and in communities, and we have trained high school students through our work with the Llano Grande Center to identify, collect, and process narratives (Guajardo & Guajardo, 2004). Training young ethnographers in public schools has been a central component of the Center's college-preparation work. Numerous young researchers have found opportunities in higher education admissions because of the kind of work they have done while in high school. With the advent of the new federal policy, No Child Left Behind, however, public schools have shifted to a strict mode of measuring every student according to quantified matrices, rather than facilitating teaching and learning processes where teachers and students find their voices (Guajardo et al., 2006) or creating spaces where they become community researchers who uncover others' silent voices (Trueba, 1989). Though public school and communities continue to respond positively to our research work, we also see schools' growing reluctance to invest time and energy in teaching and learning processes that are not measured by the "official" accountability system. That has become an increasing problem.

Community and Llano Grande

We find much of our strength in the networks that we have built. Clearly, the familial network is our core, and the influence of our parents has been critical. Our family network is also at the center of our work. Our brothers, parents, spouses, and children have been part of program development, research, and community development initiatives in which we have taken part since we have been in formal educational environments. Our dissertation defenses provide an interesting example of how our families have been involved.

First Person Commentary—Miguel

When I defended my dissertation in the summer of 2002, more than 30 people attended, 20 of them family members. As I defended, one of my brothers recorded the event on video.

First Person Commentary—Francisco

When I defended mine in 2003, 35 family members attended as well as some former high school students and other community members. The faculty committees may have been surprised to see such large crowds, but it was important to us and important to our families that we all be part of the work and the celebration.

The most important professional network that has supported and even sustained our work is the product of an organization we founded while we both taught in the public schools. The creation of the Llano Grande Center for Research and Development has been a manifestation of a sustained conversation we had been engaged in with friends who shared a similar vision of community revitalization through educational empowerment since we were teenagers. As kids growing up in a rural border town, we felt a deep connection to community. Townsfolk took great interest and pride in the school-related activities of youth, and elders and others typically supported and protected these interests. This reality influenced the nature and quality of our conversations with peers about education and community life. The conversations we nurtured beginning in the early 1980s influenced our decision to return home after college, but they also gave shape to a particular consciousness for local youth about the value of community.

Soon after our return to Edcouch-Elsa, we led an ambitious college placement effort where E-E HS students began to gain admission into Ivy League and other exclusive universities across the country. But after several years of sending dozens of talented students to these colleges, it became increasingly apparent that this work looked more like an exercise in exportating talent, than it did a community development program. We certainly did not want to participate in what is called the brain drain, which especially plagues rural communities. So we responded to the growing concern by initiating an oral history project. Before the oral history project, the college preparatory work functioned without any significant community education or awareness effort. The oral histories, we believed, would expose high school students to the stories of local elders (Guajardo & Guajardo, 2002). As students engaged in this learning process, they would also gain a new awareness of their hometown, by taking part in writing the narrative of their community. To formalize the college prep, oral history, and other community-based programming, we founded the Llano Grande Center at E-E HS in 1997.

Through the Center, the idea we imagined 20 years before is now being realized. It is important to note that, beyond the youth development and community awareness work coming out of the Center, a critical result has been formation of a network of people committed to the common mission of revitalizing the spirit and hope of our community. That network has been an essential part of how we have negotiated and survived the sometimes-difficult higher education culture. The youth and community development work that define the purpose of the Center is at the core of our research agenda as university professors. We write about it; we present the experiences at academic conferences; and we continue to provide leadership for the ongoing work. The Center is staffed by young professionals who were raised in the same rural place as we. Their dreams were nurtured as teenage students when they worked on youth leadership and community-based research initiatives. They graduated from high school, and then after graduating from Yale, Brown, Columbia, Tufts, UT–Pan American, UT–Austin, and other colleges, they returned to rural South Texas to help fuel the passions of other youth. This is the public good in which we are invested, and it is the work that stirs our passions as well.

Synthesis and Impact

We have worked to create spaces where both the public good and academia can coexist. We have done this because we've had good mentoring, but also because we feel a need to respond to the shifting demographics and changing needs of our community. We have learned that, to negotiate the spaces within institutions, we must develop a strong foundation in the communities we are serving, the work we are doing, and the lives we live. There is a natural and historical tension between the values and cultural practices of the university and those of traditional communities. A public intellectual must understand how to create, negotiate, and use power in a relational manner. To nurture this coexistence, we must respond to and live by a value system that we understand and that has proven to be effective over time; we must be able to nurture strong relationships within our community; and we must always work to create sound practices that are informed by history and research and grounded in sound theoretical practices.

We are junior faculty in institutions and academic departments that say they value the public work we engage in, but only time will tell if the balancing of our public work with the needs of the institution yields satisfactory results for both the institution and us. Of course, if the results are not positive, then we will not survive in the academy. The only thing we know for certain is that the foundation for our values, our work, and commitment to building strong community originated at home, and these elements will continue to inform our work. This is really the only thing over which we have some control, but there is little doubt that future terrain for this work is fertile and very much needed in our *comunidades*. This will fuel communities and public intellectuals who need a strong foundation within the academy.

References

Bohm, D. (1996). *On Dialogue*. London: Routledge.

Freire, P. (1970). *Pedagogy of the oppressed*. New York: Continuum.

Guajardo, José A. (1986). *Anécdotas de la vida de José Angel Guajardo: Por insistencia de Francisco Guajardo*. Unpublished manuscript.

Guajardo, F., Perez, D., Ozuna, J., Guajardo, M., Davila, E., & Casaperalta, N. (2006, October–December). Youth voice and the Llano Grande Center. *International Journal of Leadership in Education, 9*(4), 359–362.

Guajardo, M. A., & Guajardo, F. J. (2002). Critical ethnography and community change. In Y. Zou. & H. T. Trueba (Eds.), *Advances in ethnographic research: From our theoretical and methodological roots to post-modern critical ethnography*. Lanham, MD: Rowman & Littlefield.

Guajardo, M. A., & Guajardo, F. J. (2004). The impact of Brown on the brown of South Texas: A micropolitical perspective on the education of Mexican Americans in a small rural community. *American Educational Research Journal: SIA, 41*, 501–526.

Kretzmann, J. P., & McKnight, John. (1993). *Building communities from the inside out: A path toward finding and mobilizing a community's assets*. Chicago: Acta Publications.

McNeil, Linda. (2000). *Contradictions of school reform: Educational costs of standardized testing*. New York: RoutledgeFalmer.

Padilla, R. (2005). High-stakes testing and educational accountability as social constructions across cultures. In A. Valenzuela (Ed.), *Leaving children behind: How "Texas-style"accountability fails Latino youth* (pp. 249–262). Albany, NY: SUNY Press.

Padilla, R. V. (1993). Using dialogical research methods in group interviews. In D. L. Morgan (Ed.), *Successful focus group methods: Advancing the state of an art* (pp. 153–166). Newbury Park, CA: Sage.

Pizarro, M. (2001). Chicano/a power: Epistemology and methodology for social justice and empowerment in Chicano communities. *International Journal of Qualitative Studies in Education, 11*, 57–80.

Trueba, E. T. (1989). *Raising silent voices: Educating the linguistic minorities for the 21st century*. New York: Newbury House.

Valenzuela, Angela. (2005). *Leaving children behind: How "Texas-style"accountability fails Latino youth*. Albany, NY: SUNY Press.

Villenas, S. & Moreno, M. (2001). To valerse por si misma between race, capitalism, and patriarchy: Latina mother-daughter pedagogies in North Carolina. *International Journal of Qualitative Studies in Education, 5,* 671–687.

Waite, D., Nelson, S., & Guajardo, M. (In press). Teaching and leadership for social justice and social responsibility: Home is where the struggle starts. *Journal of Educational Administration and Foundations.*

LUIS URRIETA JR.

6

AGENCY AND THE GAME OF CHANGE

Contradictions, *Conciencia*, and Self-Reflection

Luis Urrieta Jr.

When I think of all that is at stake in the academy, I wonder if it is still worth doing. I wonder if this idea of change in higher education is but an illusion and if the idea of a Western notion of progress will end up consuming me. I wonder if I'll die feeling unaccomplished, co-opted, feeling like I didn't do enough, or perhaps even nothing at all.

March 2000

The question of whether we as Latina/o faculty are doing "enough" is one that plagues us and, at times, haunts us in our daily quest to struggle toward a greater good. Through formal and informal conversations with colleagues, I am often amazed by the wonderful ways Latina/o faculty work toward their goals and vision for a better world, both individually and collectively. I am also disappointed when I witness conflicts among Latinas/os that impede collaboration and create factionalism. Regardless, higher education is one arena targeted for change by Latina/o faculty, and justifiably so, since access to it has traditionally been limited in the Latina/o community. But what does it mean to struggle for change in higher education, and what do we really envision as the greater good? Are all Latina/o faculty on the same page on this issue? Perhaps a little self-reflection about the contradictions and discomfort in our lives as faculty is timely, as is our reflection on our agency and *conciencia* in this line of work.

I was recently asked to write an encyclopedia entry defining, in mostly idiomatic context, the term "sell outs" (Urrieta, forthcoming). This invitation came to me after presenting some of my work on the issue of "Playing the Game versus Selling Out" among Chicana/o activist educators (Urrieta, 2003a, 2005). The presentation was interesting as I talked to an audience of mostly young undergraduate scholars of color, predominantly African Americans. I noticed that many paid close attention to what I was saying about this issue in my work. I was also intrigued later by a particular question directed to me by a young woman in the audience. She asked, "Are you saying that because we want to be professionals in our fields and gain some status for ourselves through higher education—then we are selling out?" She looked rather defensive, but appeared genuinely interested in my response.

At first I was puzzled by the question because that is certainly not the message I wanted to convey. If anything, I wanted to highlight the agency and possibility of infiltrating the system with the intent of changing and transforming restrictive institutional practices in higher education into more democratic spaces. I noticed that this was a sensitive issue, one that seemed accusatory, involved finger pointing, and ultimately was difficult to talk about. And, indeed, the issue of playing the game versus selling out *is* difficult to talk about and, for some people, is a cause for discomfort.

I responded by telling the student that perhaps some of the Chicanas/os I interviewed in my research would say that, indeed, to seek status and recognition exclusively for self-gain is to sell out in some ways. I, however, would not pass that sort of judgment on anyone, especially when the notion of selling out is commonly understood idiomatically, but evades a standard definition. I wanted to reassure her that my intent was to highlight the importance and need to reflect on what the concept of playing the game means in terms of agency, strategizing, and working actively for social change. I assured her that this is a complex and dichotomous issue as traditionally understood, and that my most important goal was to bring attention to the issue of agency and how different people, individually and collectively, strategize to bring about change by working within institutions.

When we think about the issue of selling out and playing the game, critically and self-reflectively, it forces us to ask hard questions about our personal commitments and our priorities in the work that we do and for what we believe to be the public good and civic mission of higher education. This is not an issue of finger pointing, or about creating a list of who is and who isn't a Sell Out. If anything, by using this as a theoretical concept, what

I intend to do is shift how we traditionally think about this issue, to highlight why self-reflection is important even when it causes discomfort, and how we exert and can potentially strategize our agency, *con conciencia*, in our daily practices as faculty with a vision of service to the public good, yet working within whitestream[1] institutions.

White Supremacy and Higher Education

Different notions of what the public or greater good means exist in society. It is believed that higher education institutions are meant to be public spaces for the betterment of society, and that their product, higher education, is meant to produce engaged citizens committed to active participation for the public good. This vision, however, begs for more interrogation. Do all communities define the "public good" in the same way? Is one community's good, another community's bad? Do all communities benefit equally and equitably by way of this definition in a White supremacist system?

I would argue that not all communities share the same vision of the public good, because U.S. society was founded and continues to function under a system of White supremacy. Urrieta and Reidel (2006) define white supremacy as the official and unofficial practices, principles, morals, norms, values, history, and overall culture that privilege Whites in U.S. society. Current U.S. higher education was founded in this system, and the culture that has evolved as part of this system is filled with rituals and practices that restrict the access to these institutions of higher education, especially to the poor and people of color.

Harris's (1993) legal analysis of Whiteness as property is helpful to understand how White identity and Whiteness function to ascribe racial privilege and status to predominantly White higher education institutions. Historically and legally, only White possession and occupation of land was justified, and Whiteness was subsequently privileged as the basis for property

---

[1] Sandy Grande (2000) refers to "whitestream" as the cultural capital of Whites in almost every facet of U.S. society. Grande uses the term whitestream, as opposed to mainstream, in an effort to decenter Whiteness as dominant. Whitestream, according to Claude Denis (1997), is a term that plays on the feminist notion of "malestream." Denis defines whitestream as the idea that while (Canadian) society is not completely White in sociodemographic terms, it remains principally and fundamentally structured on the basis of the Anglo-European White experience. Whitestream in this article therefore refers to the official and unofficial texts and institutions in the United States that are founded on the practices, principles, morals, values, and history of White supremacy. I must clarify that the whitestream is not exclusively the domain of Whites in U.S. society, but of any person actively promoting white models as "standard."

rights. Because White identity and Whiteness were sources of privilege, they became exclusionary and legally protected. Examples of this protection in higher education have been the legal cases favoring the regressive goals and progress of affirmative action.

Predominantly White and middle-class institutions in a White supremacist system enjoy privileged status property (Urrieta, 2006). In other words, according to Harris (1993), higher status is a "property" of Whiteness and comes with a reputation of objectivity, high quality, justice, rigor, and goodness, to name a few attributes. Examples of this in higher education include ranking institutions using the tier-ranking system or by way of such code words as "good school" or "rigorous program." The ascription of unearned privilege to White middle-class and elite universities results in greater access to symbolic and economic resources that benefit and perpetuate White supremacy because whitestream society is more likely to invest in these schools.

When analyzing the necessity for race-based educational policy, such as affirmative action, which takes into account historical and contemporary racism, it is important to understand, as Harris (1993) aptly points out, that color blindness is a form of race subordination. Of special consideration, historically, is the use of racial categories to exclude people of color, and the condemnation of racial categories when used for resource redistribution and full inclusion purposes, such as with affirmative action (Harris, 1993, p. 1766). Color-blind education policy, such as the argument against affirmative action, does not function equally or equitably in a White supremacist system.

For those committed to dismantling White supremacy and the white-stream norms of higher educational institutions, the practice of Chicana/o, Latina/o agency and *conciencia* through the process of self-reflection can contribute to further developing a common understanding of higher education for the public good. That is what my goal is in this chapter, to call for further self-reflection among Latina/o faculty using the "playing the game" metaphor to question common understandings of higher education for the public good, even among ourselves. As a point of departure toward that goal, however, it is important to understand that we live in a White supremacist and patriarchal society from which our notions of whitestream practices as main-stream practices emerge. And since most of us work within this system, what role or roles do we each play in both sustaining and disrupting this system? Again, this is not meant as an accusatory question, but as a positive way of self-reflection about our agency and strategizing for change.

Methodology

The data for this chapter were gathered through personal, self-reflective field notes; poetry; and other documents such as syllabi, publications, and essays written over the course of six years (1999–2005). Using an autoethnographic method of data collection, the goal was to document the concrete and detailed experiences of my life as an academic (Ellis & Bochner, 2000). Emotion and self-examination using a dialectical process of reflection and internal dialogue and deliberation were important to this research (Urrieta, 2003b). A reflexive analysis was used to analyze these data as I used the experience of field work with Chicana/o activist educators to learn more about and reflect upon myself and my practices (Davies, 2001).

Dilemmas, Self-Reflection, and Becoming

Over the past six years, I've found that I am my research and my work is part of who I am as well, but it took me a long time to figure this out. In essence, the work I produce is what I consider scholarship related to my vision of a better world—my version of the public good. But I used to struggle with whether I was being co-opted by the whitestream and wondered if I was selling out in the process of becoming a researcher. I wondered if I was contributing to maintaining the status quo that perpetuates White supremacy. I had, to some extant, bought into the idea that objectivity is possible, and that perhaps by studying people like me and by following my political agendas for change, I was not being truly objective. I was not being liberated nor was I liberating. Perhaps, I was fooling myself.

> Back in my room the interrogation continues, what change do I want to see in this world? What changes do I want to make? And is it worth it? Sofia Villenas's Chicana colonizer/colonized dilemma has got to be more than the colonized reflecting on her colonization. But right now I can't think beyond that, no matter how much we'd like to think we are "liberated," "emancipated," or creating a "new discourse," the fact is that every detail of our existence is nothing more than colonial social constructions. I can almost imagine that we are fooling ourselves by thinking that the end of oppression is coming, like the slaves who celebrated their freedom, not suspecting that only a new form of slavery would replace the one they knew too well.
>
> March 2000

As this quotation shows, I struggled with the socialization process of becoming a researcher. I didn't have a big issue with the agency in teaching; the work of Paulo Freire (1970) had already inspired me to teach for critical consciousness as a former middle school teacher, but research in the academy was difficult to make peace with. I wanted to feel that my research, like my teaching, was going to accomplish something and elicit an immediate response. I hoped that I would be liberated from my own guilt in the process of research and scholarship, but somehow that solution seemed to me the easy way out. I wanted to struggle some more with the process, even if I lost sleep over it. In retrospect, my naiveté controlled my thinking. I wanted a revolution, an immediate, huge, and permanent change. Somehow, along my path, however, I learned that a revolution of the magnitude I wanted was not likely to happen. The time for a revolution, the kind of revolution I wished for, had not arrived yet.

At the same time, however, I knew that I needed to represent myself and my people through the writing process. I had read many "studies" and articles that depicted such an erroneous image of Latinas/os, especially about why so many of us don't do well in school, that I wondered . . . no . . . I demanded to know why I couldn't tell my own story—the story that I saw through my brown eyes.

> Today I saw my family in a documentary film. It wasn't really "my" family, but one very similar to mine. As I sat in my anthropology class and watched, I felt a knot form in my sore throat. I saw an *Oaxaqueño* and his family struggling to make a "better" life in California. I saw myself in every one of the scenes and in every one of the characters. . . . That was the beginning of this idea about writing my story. Was it not right for me to speak on my own behalf? Was it not right for me to write about myself? When my family is in anthropologists' ethnographies already, had I no right to say anything? I am writing this as a testimony of my existence. I want to give witness to my experiences, not just as a person of color living in the United States, but, most important, as the ethnographer I am being trained to become in the academy. As a researcher, I feel compelled to let others know what it feels like for me to see myself written on the pages of books and on television screens that I did not write and I did not produce.
>
> April 2000

This need to speak about and for myself brought up important questions about scholarship and the ways people use and misuse research. Being self-reflective I asked: What kind of scholarship did I want to produce? How would others use my work? Would it have an impact on the world beyond the academy? Would I reveal too much in it? How would it benefit Latina/o communities?

Through a brief but valuable conversation with a Native American colleague and mentor, it became clearer to me that the politics of representation carries with it a huge responsibility. The production of knowledge is not neutral, just as teaching is not neutral. That conversation had a similar effect on me as when I first read Freire. I thus began to come to peace with research and scholarship, and, most important, I began to take responsibility for representing people with dignity and pride—I came to understand the power of writing. I was part of a select number of people who had been successful despite the system's barriers set up to stop me—how could I not take this opportunity to represent seriously?

Notably and subsequently, the most powerful methodology literature I came across was in the subfield of native anthropology. The work of African American anthropologist Delmos Jones (1970) was key in shaping my ideas about research and my role as a native ethnographer.

> A practical merit of native anthropology is the access one has to one's self-identified community or communities, which is not always guaranteed; thus, generating the dilemmas. Another merit is the different, optimally more egalitarian collaboration that can potentially exist between researcher and consultants, aided by the fact that one's informants might also be one's family, friends, and long-term acquaintances, although this may also create dilemmas. Because of the native anthropologist's multi-culturality and role as cultural mediator, the native researcher is able to reflect on the self vis-à-vis his other selves, basically as a reflection of his multiple existences.
>
> May 2003

Through this literature I was exposed to works that validated my purposes and the contributions that I could make in education. I could be a researcher and maintain my dignity. I also began to remember the powerful works that greatly affected my life and practice—Freire, Villenas, Anzaldúa, Gándara, García, Holland, etc. If those works had not been written, would I think the way I do now?

Agency and Playing the Game

> This idea of a game is starting to make more sense to me now. It's like trying to win at chess. If I make this move, then what move can and will my opponent make? How will this other move either enable me to or stop me from making that other move? All of this is important . . . I'm just starting to realize it. If someone were to introduce a mathematical formula to all of this and measure potential outcomes of individual and collective agency, what would it look like? If they can do this with robots with artificial intelligence, imagine how much more effective this could be for humans with a consciousness and for the struggle for change?!
>
> September 2004

One of the most significant things in my development as a faculty member and in the struggle for social justice is the process of reflection, not just self-reflection, but also deep thinking about my research and teaching. It is not an accident that I chose a reflexive analysis to analyze the data in this chapter. An example in teaching that I recorded in field notes and that immediately came to mind is when my White students questioned me about why I always infused issues of race into my curricula and teaching. I reflected on this issue, which really was more of an accusation, while waiting for a airplane flight:

> So, why do I talk about race . . . perhaps because I get racialized in countless and different ways. Even if I pretend that race doesn't matter, I get reminded that it does every single day of my life. For me to perpetuate your imaginary perfect world is to do you a disservice, to keep you blind to your own White reality. Race is everywhere and in action all the time. You tend not to see it, pretend not to see it, or don't want to see it because to recognize it questions your authority, your privilege, your sense of entitlement. And in the logic (acknowledged or unacknowledged) of your world, that makes perfect sense. Why would you want to? It makes you uncomfortable, it makes you feel uneasy, it makes you feel angry, it makes you feel guilty. So how would you like to feel that way every single day? And you're right, it's not your fault, you didn't create this system, you were born into it, but so was everyone else! The question for you is, what are you going to do about it? So why do I talk about race? I do it because it is part of my reality at all times, and also of yours, whether you like it or not, wish to see it or not. Yes, that, too, is your privilege, to see it or not to see

it, to open your eyes to it, or to keep them closed. In my reality, I don't have that privilege—I can't be blind to it even when sometimes I wish I could be . . .

September 2003

By reflecting on these data and my teaching experience, I realized that my teaching is not divorced from my research and my commitments to Latina/o, Chicana/o communities, my politics, and, ultimately, from myself. *Concientemente*, I was willing to pay the price of keeping my dignity in teaching, even if it meant that I received negative and emotionally destructive course evaluations and being perceived by my White colleagues as a "bad" teacher.

In terms of research, I used the experience of field work with Chicana/o activist educators to learn more about and reflect upon my *conciencia* and my practices as a teacher and researcher. My research has made me genuinely interested in questioning my motives and reflecting on my engagement with power. When I was conducting interviews for my dissertation, informant after informant used the metaphor of playing the game to talk about agency, motivation, and strategy to work for social change.

The majority of Chicana/o activist educators I interviewed saw the institutional practices they negotiated as a high-stakes, highly political game and their agency as the capacity to play or participate in that game, but with the alternative motive of changing the game, or at least modifying its rules. Once the game's rules were understood, informants reported making conscious and strategic decisions about how and when to participate, or at least to disrupt the game. Moment-to-moment interactions were important because there was never an accurate prediction about when the opportunity to disrupt the game would arise. Recall that hegemony is not perfect or total; in the imperfections lie both the possibility for change to disrupt the hegemony as well as the possibility to maintain it, and sometimes that direction depends on our creative and ready ability to strategize or improvise for change.

By reflecting on my data and the publication of " 'Playing the Game' versus 'Selling Out': Chicanas' and Chicanos' Relationship to Whitestream Schools" (Urrieta, 2005), again I've understood that the games of whitestream schools, including higher education, are about power. Because the games are about power, the rules are rather arbitrary because to spell out the rules explicitly would mean that they could not be changed easily to protect

White privilege or to limit access to power. These games, from the Chicana/ o informants' perspective in my research, were at odds with the greater good and caused more damage than good to those outside the protection of Whiteness. The subjectivity of "public good" is thus disguised strategically as objectivity using a color-blind and disabling discourse that, as Harris (1993) argues, is a form of race subordination.

This understanding of the restrictive, biased, and gatekeeping cultural practices of education (e.g., admissions processes, graduate school rites of passage, and the tenure and promotion process, etc.) is not naïve at all, but rather complex and, in my perspective, accurate. To perform in this game with alternative motives and yet to make it appear that the motive to follow certain rules is innocent requires a high degree of performative and improvisational skills as well as logical, strategic awareness—a Chicana/o activist *conciencia*—of when to say what and to whom, and when to do what and for what reason. In a forthcoming work (Urrieta, Mendez, & Benavídez, 2007), I have defined Chicana/o activist *conciencia* as involving not only active awareness of one's agency in moment-to-moment interactions in the struggle for social justice, but also the responsibility to seize and plan for those moments to act in the world.

To participate in the system, or game of whitestream universities, should be considered dangerous because of the possibility of being co-opted, and because of the constant negotiation and compromise that occurs between expectations of the game and our own personal motives. However, infiltrating that system with personal dignity is necessary as long as the rules of these games are never normalized and accepted as "that's the way things are done." Rules can be followed with alternative motives if such action can lead to a greater end.

Playing the Game and the Public Good

A critical and complete assessment of one's agency in the game is indispensable, however, for all faculty members with a social justice orientation. Latina/o, Chicana/o faculty, especially those seeking a greater good, must be aware of what our goals are and what we are doing, *concientemente*, to achieve those goals. Our *conciencia* must never be "turned off" or on vacation, because being alert at every moment is important; we never know when the opportunity will arise to disrupt whitestream practices.

It is true that often and traditionally, as Chicana/o, Latina/o faculty, we have mobilized in reactive ways, but we most certainly should mobilize and strategize in proactive ways as well. By reactive ways, I refer to responding to the attacks made on us by those who do not support our efforts to increase demographic and theoretical diversity and access to higher education. By proactive ways, I refer to the multiple ways we can individually and collectively improvise, create networks and alliances, and form sustainable outlets and resources to work toward attaining our goals.

If we are aware of our agency in this and other complex ways in this game, then we must accept that we are playing dangerously by choice because we are willing to take risks to bring about change that others may not. We must embrace the idea that we have agency and are not just the victims of whitestream oppression. It is also important to realize that we exist in contradiction and that we have the opportunity to exercise our agency even in what may appear to be contradictory ways. By surrendering our hopes for change to self-defeat, loss of hope, or unconscious participation in the game, we are accepting as truth that injustices occur because "that's the way it [the system] is" and we would subsequently limit our agency to "there's nothing I/we can do about it."

My proposition is that we begin to use this, at times, oppressive and divisional dichotomy of playing the game versus selling out to help us self-reflect, both individually and collectively, about our goals and practices—not just as an either/or extreme, but also about the gray area of possibility between the two extremes. If we, as Latina/o faculty are all playing in this game of higher education with the motivation to change it for the public good, then we must ask ourselves seriously exactly *why* we are playing, with *whom* we are playing, and, most important, *how* we are playing. Each of us should literally ask him- or herself, what will my next move for social change be? If this (hypothetical) situation were to occur, how would I respond? How many people nationally would I be able to count on?

We should collectively discuss and deliberate about what our goals and visions for the public good in higher education are. Is our collective vision for higher education for the public good one that seeks to replace the current model with a similarly oppressive one, or will it genuinely be one that benefits people in our society? I am not referring here to a simplistic, color-blind way of pursuing equality and naively helping all people as if we were all really treated equally, but of critically and ethically reflecting on how higher education for the public good would benefit people who are not protected by the property of Whiteness. Asking ourselves about how we play the game with the goal of disrupting the culture and practices of White supremacy, and using this concept seriously in dialogue for and about our goals for change, would be a step in the right direction.

References

Davies, C. A. (2001). *Reflexive ethnography: A guide to researching selves and others.* London: Routledge.

Denis, C. (1997). *We are not you: First nations and Canadian modernity.* Vancouver, BC, Canada: Broadview Press, Collection Terra Incognita.

Ellis, C., & Bochner, A. B. (2000). Autoenthography, personal narrative, reflexivity: Researcher as subject. In N. K. Denzin & Y. S. Lincoln (Eds.), *Handbook of qualitative research* (2nd ed., pp. 733–768). Thousand Oaks: Sage.

Freire, P. (1970). *Pedagogy of the oppressed.* New York: Continuum.

Grande, S. M. A. (2000). American Indian geographies of identity and power: At the crossroads of Indígena and Mestizaje. *Harvard Educational Review, 70*(4), 467–498.

Harris, C. (1993). Whiteness as property. *Harvard Law Review, 106*(8), 1709–1791.

Jones, D. (1970). Towards a native anthropology. *Human Organization, 29,* 251–259.

Urrieta, L., Jr. (2003a). *Orchestrating the selves: Chicana and Chicano negotiations of identity, ideology, and activism in education.* Unpublished dissertation, University of North Carolina at Chapel Hill.

Urrieta, L., Jr. (2003b). *Las identidades también lloran*/Identities also cry: Exploring the human side of indigenous Latina/o identities. *Educational Studies, 34*(2), 147–168.

Urrieta, L., Jr. (2005). "Playing the game" versus "selling out": Chicanas' and Chicanos' relationship to whitestream schools. In B. K. Alexander, G. Anderson, & B. Gallegos (Eds.), *Performance theories in education: Power, pedagogy, and the politics of identity* (pp. 173–196). Mahwah, NJ: Lawrence Erlbaum.

Urrieta, L., Jr. (2006). Community identity discourse and the Heritage Academy: Colorblind educational policy and white supremacy. *International Journal of Qualitative Studies in Education, 9*(4), 455–476.

Urrieta, L., Jr. (forthcoming). Sell outs. In W. A. Darity (Ed.), *International Encyclopedia of the Social Sciences* (2nd ed.) Farmington Hills, MI: Macmillan References USA.

Urrieta, L., Jr., & Méndez Benavídez, L. (2007). Community commitment and activist scholarship: Chicano professors and the practice of consciousness. *Journal of Hispanic Higher Education, 6,* 222–236..

Urrieta, L., Jr., & Reidel, M. (2006). Avoidance, anger, and convenient amnesia: White supremacy and self-reflection in social studies teacher education. In E. Wayne Ross (Ed.), *Race, Ethnicity, and Education.* Westport, CT: Praeger.

CAROLINE SOTELLO VIERNES TURNER

7

TOWARD PUBLIC EDUCATION AS A PUBLIC GOOD[1]

Reflections from the Field

Caroline Sotello Viernes Turner

Picking tomatoes and cutting apricots with my family in California, I played games and scenarios in my mind to keep me otherwise occupied. I never dreamed of becoming a professor or even going to college. I grew up doing field work and now, as a qualitative researcher, I find it amusing that I still find myself doing field work.

I became a researcher with a focus on access and equity in higher education because I knew how important those issues are to my home community. I am a woman of color[2] from a "no collar" laborer class. I grew up as part of a large immigrant family living and working on farm labor camps in the agricultural fields of rural California. My family and extended families had an abiding faith in the importance and accessibility of public education for their children. My parents would always encourage us to go to

---

[1] "The term public good is often used to refer to goods that are nonexcludable as well as nonrival. This means it is not possible to exclude individuals from the good's consumption. Fresh air may be considered a public good as it is not generally possible to prevent people from breathing it" (Retrieved July 18, 2006, from http://en.wikipedia.org/wiki/Public_good). This type of good may not exist in reality but it is an ideal to strive for, particularly with regard to the concept of education as a public good.

[2] The terms "woman or man of color," "students of color," and "faculty of color" refer to persons of African American, American Indian, Asian Pacific American, and Latino origin. In using the term in this way, I understand that "people of color" do not constitute a monolithic group and recognize that Whites are also members of a distinct racial category. And, certainly, by using the individual racial and ethnic categories, I do not mean to imply that all persons so "designated" experience anything in a uniform way. Rather, these categories are used to present existing data distinguishing among these groups, identify some common themes, and make overall statements about the varying experiences of the identified groups.

school so that we could obtain a job other than that of a farm laborer. I view them as a phenomenal success in promoting education to their children. All eight of us graduated from high school, quite an accomplishment for farm labor families then and, unfortunately, even now. Now, as I think about the concept of education as a public good, I realize that we assumed public education was a public good, available and attainable for everyone. In many ways, my educational accomplishments could be pointed out as an example of how the educational system works to educate the poor and the masses. However, many of my schooling experiences and the experiences of others I have interviewed, particularly women and men of color, as well as existing data detailing varied educational attainment outcomes, point to an educational pathway fraught with barriers. These barriers paint a picture that is contrary to the concept of education as a public good. Writing this chapter gives me a chance to tell you about a few of my reflections, from childhood to the present, on barriers to, as well as facilitators of, education as a public good.

Early Years

My father was from the Philippines, and my mother was from Mexico. My father fought in World War II and was very patriotic. Every day, including weekends, he toiled in the fields from sunup to sundown. My mother became a foster child after her parents died, and she was punished if she spoke Spanish. Our family had very little in terms of material possessions and lived in corrugated steel shacks belonging to the farm's owner. It was easy for farm owners to move us quickly from one living area to another to work in different locations. Continual relocation from one place to another presented challenging barriers to school enrollment and attendance.

Regardless of the trials they endured, my mother and father did everything they could to support their children. They both felt fortunate to be in the United States, where their children would be able to attend public schools. I remember my father saying that if we had been born in the Philippines, we would have had to work in the rice fields all our lives, and that, at least, here there was free education for everyone. He would not have had any money to send me to school in his home country. I was happy that I was able to go to school, as we had no extra money; and if we had to pay for

Caroline Sotello Viernes Turner with her mother, Gabriella Sotello García

books and school fees, I might have worked in the fields of California all of my life.

I had some wonderful experiences in the small, rural elementary and high schools that I attended. Most of my school time was spent reading or doing homework. I was not very social, but was drawn to the worlds found in my textbooks and other books from the school library. When did I begin to realize that there were exclusionary factors that kept people like me from access to public education? When did I start noticing the barriers to what my family thought was a public good?

I remember the school principal telling me that, while I had done well in elementary school, high school was different. He ended his statement

Caroline Sotello Viernes Turner in grade school

with, "You people marry early and have kids." I thought this was a strange thing to say but did not really pay attention to the comment. I believe the first time I noticed that I was not welcome in a class was in high school. My counselor helped me set up a schedule of classes, and I was placed in the college preparatory track. I had no idea what that meant, but I accepted the slate of classes and went to the first one, which was geography. The teacher saw me and immediately said that I was not in the right class. I went back to my counselor who brought me back to the class and informed the teacher that I was in the correct class. I was the only farm laborer in the class and the only non-White student. The first few days I knew that I was being tested to see if I truly belonged.

One day the teacher asked me to take a piece of chalk and label where the Pacific Ocean was on a map. I went up to the board and wrote Pacific Ocean in the correct location. I felt good until the teacher yanked the chalk from my fingers and admonished me for having written Pacific Ocean too small, and then he wrote it in very big letters. I could only think that the Pacific Ocean was so big that no one could write as big as it was. I sat down and could tell that some of the other students were embarrassed for me. I loved learning, so I kept up with my studies and recall doing well in the end. I had earned my place in the college preparatory track. I wonder, though, what made me persevere; others might have been so intimidated that they might have frozen up and decide not to participate in education at all, or they might have retreated to places in the curriculum where we were more represented, so there would at least be comfort in numbers. Some of my friends fought against the prejudices they encountered. Their complaints were ignored, and they were expelled from school for their disruptive behavior.

Several factors kept me in classes where I was an outsider and therefore destined to be a loner. I remember classmates making plans to get together after school, but I was not part of their circle, so I was not invited. Even if I had been, my parents would never have let me go. I had to come right home after school. I remained engaged in school because I loved learning and reading. I was so good at these skills that I received praise from everyone, including my parents. I remember one day when my father told me that I was smart and could do anything I wanted to do. I remembered his words, especially when others said the opposite to me. I did not realize it at the time, but those words served as a shield for me; they were like a suit of impenetrable armor. This was very important, as I was to encounter other challenging transitions moving from high school to college and to the professoriate.[3]

My experiences, some of which I describe here, make me realize how fortunate I was to have some confidence in my abilities when I encountered educational barriers based on stereotypes regarding my ethnic, racial, gender, and class background. However, this should not be the case if education truly serves the public good. Educators must strive to instill confidence in all students so they can develop their talents. Devaluing student potential and the knowledge students bring to the classroom from their communities makes them feel that they are not *a part of* the educational process but *apart from* it. Their hopes and dreams unrealized, many may opt to leave school. This is a loss to the individuals involved and to society as a whole.

In my case, some teachers and other supporters along the way helped me to take part in and enjoy public education. In high school, I had great biology and language teachers, who offered me a chance to stay after school and help set up projects for the next day as well as assist with correcting papers. These opportunities typically took place after school, and I could stay as long as I wanted, provided I did not miss the bus home. There were positives and negatives to having strict parents. On the one hand, I stayed focused and did what I needed to do to receive high grades. In fact, I was salutatorian when I graduated. I received some Bs in physical education, which kept me from being valedictorian. On the other hand, even if I wanted to, I could not stay after school to help my teachers and participate in after-school sports and other activities.

A dedicated and caring teacher took it upon herself to make sure that I applied to college and received a scholarship, so, after high school graduation, I left home to attend the University of California at Davis. I was the only graduate from my farm labor community to go to the university. I went to college and stayed in college, thanks to the support of my family, extended family, and inspiring educators. After I completed my undergraduate and master's degrees, almost 20 years passed before I received my Ph.D. In the late 1960s, I was hired as one of the first counselors for UC Davis's Educational Opportunity Program (EOP) and began to work in programs supporting the entrance of low-income racial and ethnic minority students into

---

[3] I have written about some of these experiences in other papers (Turner, 1994, 2000a, 2002b; Turner, Harris, & García, 2006).

higher education. I was also married and raising a family. In the early 1980s, I enrolled at Stanford University in a doctoral program as a single parent with two children.

I was very happy in my role as an EOP counselor. I believe this is one way to contribute to the public good—by participating in efforts to support inclusion of all who want to attain postsecondary education. My work as a doctoral student and as a faculty member, in the years that followed, was to focus on ways to provide some understanding of the barriers and facilitators that affect the educational participation of low-income students and/or students of color on college campuses. In my view, working to include all potential participants in postsecondary education is work to promote education as a public good. Education, which plays a critical role in helping people to realize their dreams and to develop their talent(s) to the fullest, contributes to the sustainability of a diverse and democratic society. In my work as a college student affairs administrator and, later, as a faculty member, I attempted and continue to develop, as well as participate in, research, scholarship, and service that directly examines the role of education and its service to the public.[4]

Doctoral Student

I knew I was the only or one of just a few Latina/Filipina students in my high school college preparatory classes as well as in my college courses, but I did not realize the unique space the EOP students I advised and I inhabited in higher education until I began to look at state and national data reporting our severe underrepresentation on college campuses. For example, as a doctoral student, I examined the transfer rates of Latina/o students from two-year to four-year colleges. If they do graduate from high school, many Latina/o students begin their postsecondary education in two-year colleges close to the communities in which they grew up. Few minority students, especially women, Latinas, and Filipinas, attend college far from home. In this way, I was also different. I left home and went to college far from my family. I was

---

[4] According to the 2006 American Educational Research Association (AERA) conference theme, Education Research in the Public Interest, "Education researchers are positioned to help reinvigorate the discourse and the investment in the public good by offering research and scholarship that directly look at education and the public . . . " (Retrieved July 18, 2006, from http://www.aera.net/annualmeeting/?id = 694).

not able to see them except during holidays during most of my time in college. Unfortunately, transfer rates to four-year colleges were, and continue to be, extremely low for students of color.

As part of my doctoral dissertation, I interviewed Latina/o students and, from their perspective, learned about their experience with the transfer process. Most of these students did not understand how to navigate their postsecondary educational experience. For example, while expressing interest in going to a four-year college, they were not enrolled in transfer programs and/or courses. In addition, community college campuses with high Latina/o student enrollment appeared to offer few opportunities for student transfer.[5]

Many of these community college students had backgrounds similar to mine, and I learned so much about my own experience as I reflected on what they told me about their educational experiences. The importance of learning the vocabulary and practices of an alien environment to survive and thrive was evident in student narratives. I had to make similar adaptations to succeed in college. At the same time, interviews with Latina/o students underscored the need for students like us to develop an awareness of and appreciation for what we contribute, from our experiences and perspectives, to the learning process. Everyone has expertise and cultural capital to add to the classroom experience. Conducting this study and listening to these students prompted me to define my role as an educator as that of a facilitator, nurturing the development of all students and building their confidence in their abilities and talents. In turn, I remain open to learning from each person enrolled in my classes.

Faculty Work

As a doctoral candidate, I was hired as an assistant professor at the University of Minnesota, the first Latina/Filipina assistant professor in a tenure-track position in my department. I did not realize that I was a first at the time of my hire, but a senior colleague, who kept abreast of the numbers of Latina/o scholars hired as faculty, pointed this out to me. He said, "So if you feel alone, you are alone." I also was the first Latina/Filipina to obtain tenure and a full professorship in that department.

---

[5] See Turner, 1990, 1992. The 1990 article was published in a journal that no longer exists. If you would like a copy, please e-mail the author at csturner@asu.edu.

For the last 20 years, in my role as a faculty member at the University of Minnesota and currently at Arizona State University, I contributed and continue to contribute time to publications, research projects, and curricular development projects that further exploration of the educational experiences of women and men of color. While doing this work, I found that it is critical for faculty to mentor students and junior colleagues. In recognizing and nurturing their talents, I coauthor papers with them, make presentations with them, invite them to collaborate on various research projects, encourage them to compete for dissertation fellowships/early career awards, and provide advice and support. Many of these students and junior faculty have moved on to become professionals and/or have secured tenured positions in academe. While I try to mentor students and junior faculty, they, in turn, have supported and continue to support me in all the work I do. My ability to persist and grow in academe is, in large part, due to the critical support I receive from students and junior and senior scholars within my academic homes, in addition to the support I receive from them as I travel across the

Caroline Sotello Viernes Turner with her mentees

country and abroad for professional meetings and to make presentations on my work.

Over the last decade, while conducting research on the experiences of faculty of color in higher education, I have had many opportunities to interview, converse with, and read and write about the lives of other faculty of color. Many of these faculty, as also reflected in the community college student interviews briefly noted above, feel success in academe requires them to leave themselves, who they are, at the door of graduate education and the tenure process. Again, with faculty and graduate students, as with undergraduates, devaluing their varied cultural perspectives and failing to recognize the unique contributions they can make presents a tremendous barrier to promoting an educational process that serves the public good.

I believe that each person brings a unique background to his or her experience. Who you are shapes the types of questions you ask, the kinds of issues that interest you, and the ways in which you seek solutions. Although student and faculty socialization processes are very strong, we must not lose ourselves in the process of fitting in. One method I use to maintain a connection between my past and my present is to incorporate my personal history into my present research and teaching. For example, in oral presentations of my work, I incorporate slides of my family and the places where I grew up, connecting these experiences to my development as a scholar. The backgrounds we bring to academia need not take a back seat to our professional lives; they can and must be placed in the foreground of our work. Indeed, in doing so, we contribute to the creation of an enriched intellectual campus climate[6] and the development of a welcoming campus environment for all students, including nontraditional and less-represented students.

I consider myself a scholar advocate, as I do not want to write only to attain higher faculty rank; I want also to stimulate organizational change. Toward this end, I was given an opportunity to write a book, entitled *Diversifying the Faculty: A Guidebook for Search Committees* (Turner, 2002a). This book synthesizes research on faculty hiring and translates research findings into practical recommendations that search committee chairs and others can implement as they undertake efforts to diversify their faculties. The book has sold more than 12,000 copies and is now in its second printing. As a result of writing this book, I travel all around the country giving workshops and lectures to the many faculty and administrators who want to make a difference

---

[6] For more discussion, see Turner, 2000b.

by increasing the number of faculty of color on their campuses. I believe that many of these individuals are linking the importance of supporting quality, which includes diversity, in education with service for the public good.

For example, with regard to the contributions of a diverse professoriate, based on my empirical and personal observations and those of other scholars, the more diverse college and university faculty are, the more likely it is that all students will be exposed to a wider range of scholarly perspectives and to ideas drawn from a variety of life experiences. Contributions from faculty of varied racial and ethnic backgrounds are central to the mission of the academy, an enterprise that purports to further the interests of the common good through the free search for and interpretation of knowledge. Unfortunately, the paucity of professors of color reinforces the myth that people of color cannot be successful in academia. On the other hand, creating a community of students and teachers from different backgrounds can promote learning and potentially can dispel stereotypes through cross-racial interactions inside and outside the classroom. Encouraging diversity among students and faculty is a matter of educational quality as well as equality (Alger, 1999).

Currently, I am focusing on the career path histories of African American, Latina, Asian Pacific American, and American Indian women who are presidents of colleges and universities. While conducting a literature search on the history of ethnic women presidents, I found little written to document the lives of the first Asian Pacific American, Latina, and American Indian women presidents of four-year, baccalaureate-degree-granting colleges. These women of color firsts are still in their presidencies. Based on my initial interviews with them, I learned that they are committed to creating learning environments that welcome all students and that stimulate the development of all students, including women, people of color, and other underserved communities. These women of color firsts are making important contributions to higher education and are paving the way for others to follow—others who see in these women's accomplishments possibilities for themselves. I am now writing manuscripts that tell their stories and bring their accomplishments to light (Turner, 2007). They provide important examples of how one can work to fulfill the promise of education for the public good.

Much More to Accomplish

Examining data on the participation in higher education of others like me—a first-generation college-goer from a low-socioeconomic-status background and a woman, as well as a member of a racial/ethnic group referred to as a minority group—I continue to see our lack of representation. In fact, the further one rises in academe, the fewer women and men of color are present. These data point to the continued failure of higher education to serve all of its publics. Today, the pattern of low academic degree attainment, small numbers among the various faculty ranks, and even smaller numbers among high-level administrative appointments for people of color, particularly for women of color, is well documented. For example, the data in tables 7.1 and 7.2 reveal the status of women of color as students and faculty.

In addition to the data presented above detailing the low numbers of women of color obtaining a doctorate, as well as their low numbers among the full professor ranks, results of a survey reported in *The American College President* (ACE, 2002) reveal that, among all campus president respondents (2,366), 511 (21.6%) were women. Of the women, 31 (6.1%) were Hispanic, five (1%) were Asian American, seven (1.4%) were American Indian, 36 (7%) were African American, and 430 (84.1%) were White (p. 13). This report goes on to state that the "demographic profile of the typical college or university president is slowly changing but continues to be white (87%) and male (79%)" (p. 9). The report concludes that "the imperative of rapid change, including an increasing racially and socioeconomically diverse student body, suggests a need for adaptability and diversity in higher education institutions and their leaders" (p. 47).

TABLE 7.1
Women's Educational Enrollment and Attainment by Race and Ethnicity

	College Enrollment, Fall 2003 [1]	Degrees Conferred, 2003–4 [2]		
		Bachelor's	Master's	Doctorate
White, non-Hispanic	6,347,500	580,631	225,755	14,647
American Indian	105,600	6,394	2,065	127
Asian	577,600	50,713	16,605	1,339
Black, non-Hispanic	1,338,200	87,390	36,004	1,885
Hispanic	1,006,900	57,356	18,853	896
Total Women	9,644,900	804,117	329,395	23,055

[1] Source: Almanac, 2006, p. 15; information does not include foreign students. Because of rounding, details may not add up to total.
[2] Source: Almanac, 2006, p. 22; information does not include nonresident aliens.

TABLE 7.2
Full-Time Faculty Women by Race and Ethnicity, Fall 2003[3]

	Rank		
	Assistant	*Associate*	*Full*
White	52,754	41,816	34,363
American Indian	340	242	154
Asian	5,049	2,540	1,611
Black	5,188	3,341	1,916
Hispanic	2,509	1,523	957
Total Women	69,500	50,203	39,366
Total Faculty	153,064	132,961	166,415

[3] Source: Almanac, 2006, p. 26; information does not include nonresident aliens and race unknown.

Thus, as one tracks representation of women of color upward in the academic hierarchy, their numbers all but disappear at the highest levels, particularly at the full professor and senior administration levels. Data show that few women of color are in the assistant, associate, and full professor ranks, and there is a body of literature citing the myriad barriers women of color must overcome to succeed not only as faculty (Aleman, 1995; Rains, 1999; Turner, 2002b; Turner & Myers, 2000) but in senior-level administrative positions as well (Canul, 2003; Farris, 1999; Hansen, 1997; Ideta & Cooper, 1999; King, 1999; McDemmond, 1999).

Conclusion

Reflecting on these data from a personal perspective, I can see that I am one of very few Latinas/Filipinas with a doctorate, and that I am counted as one of the 957 full professors who are Hispanic women. I realize that, from my sphere of influence, I must take action to promote access and equity for students of color, increase the numbers of those attempting to obtain a doctorate, and widen the pathways for those interested in entering the professoriate and senior-level campus administration. Based on my experience as a student, staff member, and faculty member, I have observed many barriers that keep education from being a public good. Several of these barriers are based on race/ethnicity, gender, and class.

In my role as a professor and researcher, I must work to achieve the promise reflected by the phrase, "education for the public good," and strive to welcome all communities, including communities of color. This year, I was honored to hood several students, including four Latinas, one Latino, and two American Indian women who received their graduate degrees. I was glad to play a part in supporting their growth and nurturing their talents.

I realize that any efforts I make to promote education as a public good may be viewed as drops in a bucket. At times I doubt that what I am doing makes any difference because, in general, people of color continue to be almost invisible in much of the academic landscape. However, I gain inspiration from my family, friends, colleagues, and students as well as from the words of a filmmaker who notes that one grain of sand (Freidberg, 2005) can combine with others to make a difference.

References

Aleman, A. M. (1995). Actuando. In R. Padilla & R. Chavez (Eds.), *The leaning ivory tower: Latino professors in American universities.* (pp. 67–76). Albany, NY: State University of New York Press.

Alger, J. (1999). When color-blind is color-bland: Ensuring faculty diversity in higher education. *Stanford Law and Policy Review, 10*(2), 191–204.

Almanac. (2006). The nation: Faculty and staff. *The Chronicle of Higher Education, 53.*

American Council on Education (ACE). (2002). *The American college president.* Washington, DC: Author.

Canul, K. (2003). Latina/o cultural values and the academy: Latinas navigating through the administrative role. In J. Castellanos & L. Jones (Eds.), *The majority in the minority: Expanding the representation of Latina/o faculty, administrators and students in higher education* (pp. 167–175). Sterling, VA: Stylus.

Farris, V. (1999). Succeeding as a female African American president of a predominantly White college. In W. Harvey (Ed.), *Grass roots and glass ceilings: African American administrators in predominantly white colleges and universities* (pp. 57–69). Albany, NY: State University of New York Press.

Freidberg, J. (2005). *Granito de arena.* Seattle, WA: Corrugated Films.

Hansen, V. L. (1997). *Voices of Latina administrators in higher education: Salient factors in achieving success and implications for a model of leadership development for Latinas.* A dissertation submitted to the faculties of Claremont Graduate School and San Diego State University. UMI Microform 9805058. Ann Arbor, MI: UMI Company.

Ideta, L., & Cooper, J. (1999). Asian women leaders of higher education: Stories of strength and self discovery. In L. Christian-Smith & K. Kellor (Eds.), *Everyday knowledge and uncommon truths: Women of the academy* (pp. 129–146). Boulder, CO: Westview Press.

King, R. C. (1999). Succeeding against the odds in higher education: Advancing society by overcoming obstacles due to race and gender. In W. Harvey (Ed.), *Grass roots and glass ceilings: African American administrators in predominantly white colleges and universities* (pp. 9–37). Albany, NY: State University of New York Press.

McDemmond, M. (1999). On the outside looking in. In W. Harvey (Eds.), *Grass roots and glass ceilings: African American administrators in predominantly white colleges and universities* (pp. 71–82). Albany, NY: State University of New York Press.

Rains, F. (1999). Dancing on the sharp edge of the sword: Women faculty of color in white academe. In L. Christian-Smith & K. Kellor (Eds.), *Everyday knowledge and uncommon truths: Women of the academy* (pp. 147–173). Boulder, CO: Westview Press.

Turner, C. S. (1990, Fall). A California case study: Organizational determinants of the transfer of Hispanic students from two- to four-year colleges in the Bay area. *Metropolitan Education, 6,* 1–24.

Turner, C. S. (1992, Spring). It takes two to transfer: Relational networks and educational outcomes. *Community College Review, 19*(4), 27–33.

Turner, C. S. (1994, July–August). Alien students alien staff: How awesome the gap in higher education. *Colors: Minnesota's Journal of Opinion by Writers of Color, 4*(3), 23–27.

Turner, C. S. (2000a). Defining success: Promotion and tenure—Planning for early career stage and beyond. In M. García (Ed.), *Succeeding in an academic career: A guide for faculty of color* (pp. 11–40). Westport, CT: Greenwood.

Turner, C. S. (2000b). New faces, new knowledge. *Academe, 86*(5), 34–37.

Turner, C. S. (2002a). *Diversifying the faculty: A guidebook for search committees.* Washington, DC: Association of American Colleges and Universities.

Turner, C. S. (2002b). Women of color in academe: Living with multiple marginality. *Journal of Higher Education, 73*(1), 74–93.

Turner, C. S. (2007). Pathways to the presidency: Biographical sketches of women of color firsts. *Harvard Educational Review, 77,* 1–38.

Turner, C. S., Harris, R. G., & García, G. S. Mothers and daughters address inequities: From our spheres of influence. In L. O'Brien & B. B. Swadener (Eds.), *Writing the motherline: Mothers, daughters and education* (pp. 113–129). Lanham, MD: University Press/Rowman & Littlefield.

Turner, C. S., & Myers, S. L., Jr. (2000). *Faculty of color in academe: Bittersweet success.* Needham Heights, MA: Allyn & Bacon.

FLORA V. RODRIGUEZ-BROWN

8

FOR THE PUBLIC GOOD

A Personal Reflection

Flora V. Rodriguez-Brown

This is an autoethnography (Ellis & Bochner, 2000) presented as a personal essay in the first person. It is based on my recollection and reflection on issues of social conscience[1] and the public good. My reflections begin at childhood and span my entire career as an academic in the United States. Through this exercise, I sought to understand how I positioned myself within multiple definitions of the public good, and how I learned to play the academic game in my new country (my country of origin is Costa Rica) without losing my vision of social justice or my commitment to the community I represent, Latinos. Over more than 30 years of service in American higher education, I learned that the public good has multiple definitions, and that context and culture contribute to each definition. I believe that individuals *should* be able to integrate their personal vision of the public good with that of their universities as public institutions. This is not always the case. To succeed in academia, we need to "play the game." Playing the game should not mean, however, that we shove aside our own vision of social justice or our own social consciousness as members of ethnic communities. Some of us have been able to make it in unconventional ways, and I believe it is worthwhile to take such risks. After all, without risk and sacrifice, how can we expect any vision of social justice to be realized?

---

[1]In Spanish, *conciencia social* may be translated as "social consciousness" or "social conscience." I have chosen to use "conscience" here because it implies action.

Learning at Home . . . and Enjoying Life

My story is different from that of many participants in this project. I was born and raised in a different country, in a society some term socialist, with a large middle class and great respect for all individuals. Very early in life I learned to value everyone. I come from a very progressive family. My parents were both teachers, and it was very important to them that I be able to relate to, respect, and value all kinds of people. Costa Rica at that time was a country where you could not promote yourself as better than others. If you tried to do so, someone would find something wrong with you or your family to level the playing field.

I am the oldest of six children. I went to public school, and for the first six years of schooling, I had the same teacher, who was excellent. My siblings and I learned not only at school, but also at home, where my father planned experiential activities for the family. I learned about civics and the public good from my family and our local community. As a family, we developed community projects, which we always carried out anonymously. We spent weekends at nursing homes talking to older people and taking them for rides (in a borrowed car). I remember the happiness in those elders' eyes when they were able to go for a ride. Another project I remember took place when the street numbers were changed in my town. We got support from and gave credit to the Lions' Club in town, but it was my siblings and I who went door-to-door telling people about their new addresses. My father provided us with handmade maps showing the written address for each home. On other occasions, we collected money to buy new habits for the nuns working at the local hospital, when we saw that theirs were falling apart. We could do all of these things because life was simple and social consciousness was high. This was the benefit of living in a very small and underdeveloped country; I think of it as a big farm.

Through my parents and extended family, I also learned to live with and respect nature and the environment. I learned about animals, trees, and plants, and about life in the countryside, through long walks with my father and siblings. How lucky I was to be able to share the experience. We did not have a car; but my uncle did, and sometimes we went away to the mountains, the oceans (Pacific and Atlantic), and the valleys to explore nature and talk to people.

I cannot say that the country is the same today. It is much more populous and more developed, and its middle class is smaller. Costa Rica now has a more diverse society. Schools and family structures have changed. Doors are closed, and it is hard to know the people in your neighborhood and your town. Much of the wildlife that surrounded us when I was growing up can only be seen in nature preserves now.

Life was simple and good, but life with my parents did not last long. My father had a car accident and later died of cancer when I was 14. My youngest sibling was two years old at the time, and my mother tried to be both mother and father for us, providing for us the best she could. We were all good students. When I graduated from high school, I was able to go to the University of Costa Rica on a government scholarship. To do so, you had to take an admissions exam. If you passed the exam, you could attend the university and pay according to your parents' income. I went there for free. During the four years I attended the university, I earned a bachelor's degree in education and took two years of chemistry. Then I was offered the opportunity to compete for a scholarship to study in the United States, which is how I became a foreign student at the University of Illinois at Urbana-Champaign (UIUC) many years ago. After two years, I graduated with a bachelor's degree in chemistry and decided that, since I preferred to be involved with students and teach, I should pursue further studies in education. I was admitted to a master's in education program at the same university, and, during my first semester as a graduate student, my mother died. I was 23 years old; my youngest sibling was 11. As we (my siblings and I) were dealing with our pain and the fact that we no longer had parents or anyone to support us, we were told we could be divided up among different relatives. Instead, we decided to stay together and help each other. One sister, who was 21 and recently married, supported my idea to continue my studies here. She kept my three youngest siblings living with her, and I brought one of my sisters with me to the United States. I worked two jobs to support my sister and myself and to pay for her ESL classes so she could get a student visa.

I have to say that we were successful in helping each other. Life changed a lot. We did not have much, but we were happy, and each of us worked very hard to "become somebody" and help one another. In many ways, the public good became the "family good."

I was not aware how special my family and childhood experiences were in Costa Rica until I came to the United States. It was then that I learned about differences among people, about lack of respect for one another, and about discrimination. I also learned how little people knew about respecting and enjoying nature.

Experiences as a Student in the United States

One of the experiences I had to deal with in the United States—besides the difficulties of learning English—was the perception that students at the university had about foreign students. To them, we looked different and spoke in funny accents; but they also viewed us as wealthy "brats." It was hard to think of myself as a wealthy "brat," while I was working full time and carrying a full academic load.

I enjoyed my studies at the College of Education. In 1972, with the support of a professor and mentor, I developed what would be the first course in bilingual education at the UIUC campus. As a student, I designed this service-learning course to train school personnel in small towns to support the education of migrant children. Undergraduate students, mostly Latinos from Chicago, received credit for this course and spent two days a week in two towns about an hour from campus. We helped school personnel to translate school forms and opened communication between Latino parents and the school. In one of the towns, we stayed late into the evening to teach Spanish to the doctor, a pastor, and some of the people who employed both the migrant workers and a group of immigrants from Cadereita, Mexico, who were brought to work in a broom factory.

It was in this setting that I learned about discrimination. Although we had a lot of friends in those towns, there were also many people who did not want us there. We were limited as to where we could eat. Once, we were even accused of teaching the migrant workers to be subversive and were given five minutes to leave town. This accusation was unfounded, but I had to clear the situation with the university to keep the class going.

From my junior year as an undergraduate to the time when I finished my Ph.D. in educational psychology, I spent eight years in Urbana-Champaign. Those were good years during which I developed a sense of the common good that included serving communities with which I had a cultural and linguistic affinity. I also learned how to do academic work while pursuing my commitment to social justice.

From Foreign Student to Minority in One Day

Once you learn about how labels play a major role in U.S. society, it is easy to expect a change when you change status. It was during the sixth year of my studies in Urbana-Champaign that I got married. It did not take long for my status to change from "foreign student" to "minority student." I sensed it was coming, and I knew some of the stereotypes that accompany that label. It happened very fast, but I was prepared for it. From that day on, I decided that my vocation as a minority was to work hard and support the people I represented: Latinos in the United States. That was my vision of the public good.

My commitment to this cause has been a part of my daily life, and it is a major thrust of my academic life. In embracing my role as a Latina academic, I made it clear to my Latino friends, colleagues, and students who were born and raised in the United States that, while I might not completely understand their experiences growing up as minorities, I am socially conscious and committed to working for and with them.

What role have I played in pursuing this endeavor? It has been a balancing act of learning to play the academic game and pursuing my own understanding of the public good—an understanding quite different from those who become the conventional definition of the label "professor."

Learning to Be the Lowest on a Totem Pole . . . and Surviving While Pursuing the Public Good

Soon after I got married, and while still working on my doctoral dissertation, I took a job at a university in Chicago. It was not a tenure-track position, but rather, in a Title IV program providing services to school districts and communities around the Midwest.

My first boss was a Chicano; I learned very quickly that, as a Latina from Latin America, I was the lowest on the academic totem pole. I was discriminated against in many ways (salary, assignments, recognition), but I survived and learned. One of the first things I learned was that European Americans are not the only ones who discriminate against Latinos. There was also discrimination among Latinos themselves, which was a shame because we usually shared a similar vision of the public good.

My next academic position was with a very well-known organization that supported projects related to second-language learners. I was to be one of three principal investigators (PIs) involved in an educational project in Illinois. However, it wasn't until I accepted the job that I realized I was going to be the only person doing the data collection in the state; one of the PIs was going to be out of the country, and the other would work from another location.

There was a lot of work to be done, and coordinating the data collection for this major evaluation required a great deal of time and effort. Toward the end of the year, the three PIs agreed to divide the work and to share authorship of any publications that came out of the projects. Suddenly, and to my surprise, a paper including qualitative data that I had collected and knew well appeared in a journal in Canada without my name. When I complained, I was told that they could add my name and that it would appear as a clarification in a future issue of the journal. I did not accept this solution, and the situation opened my eyes to life in academic settings.

Another learning experience occurred when I was offered a research position as a visiting assistant professor at the University of Illinois at Chicago (UIC) College of Education in the late 1970s. At that point, I had received and was working on a grant from the National Institute of Education (NIE). When I took the job at UIC, I had my own ideas about a research agenda and was looking forward to being a part of an academic setting that would support my research endeavors. Once I took the job, however, I learned that the school did not view my commitment to do research and work with linguistic minorities, in particular with Latinos, as one of my central responsibilities. I discovered that I was hired so the dean of the college and his associates could use my skills and minority status for their benefit. They expected that I would write and apply for grants that would benefit what they determined to be the public good, which was certainly very different from my vision. I chose not to acquiesce to their expectations, and I paid a price for that choice. After three years, my job was cut from the budget and later transformed into a tenure-track position for which a minority male was hired. He left the university three years later.

Finally, a Tenure-Track Position . . . But with Extra Baggage

The academic job experiences I described above taught me not only about discrimination, but also about how the public good can be defined in different ways. From my perspective, the public good is defined in terms of the context, culture, and social consciousness of the individual. From the perspective of the institutions, the public good is defined as that which meets the needs of the institution and those who hold power within it.

My desire to work with the Latino community and contribute to the training of new teachers to better serve the needs of Latino children led me to apply for a tenure-track position at the UIC College of Education. The position required developing a program to train bilingual teachers as well as grant-writing skills, since the goal was to attract new Latino students to the college by offering them financial support from government grants.

As I think of it now, it was a tenure-track position, but with more responsibilities than other tenure-track positions for which faculty were hired at about the same time. In addition to meeting requirements for research, teaching, and service, I had to administer and develop a program, and I was expected to bring in training grants to support new Latino students. I was told that the expectations for tenure were the same for me as for other faculty members working toward tenure without such responsibilities.

Being new in academia and also new to life in the United States, I did not completely understand what I was getting into when I accepted the job. I did not think about fairness, even when I realized that other newly hired colleagues had very different academic lives from mine.

Eventually, as I developed the program, recruited students, offered academic support to students in need, and taught most of the courses in the program, I realized I did not have the time that other colleagues had for research and writing. It was then that I decided to do what I thought was right. I was not compromising my social consciousness or my private vision of the public good; I was committed to bringing more Latinos to the college, and I wanted to train teachers to serve the needs of Latino children, particularly new immigrants. It was a matter of social justice, and I was on a mission, despite the extra burden. I decided that I had to play the academic game to the best of my ability, while keeping in perspective what my minority status within the college required from me. I was working for the "public good," but my public good was defined differently from that pursued by other faculty members within the university. Was that fair? I simply did not ask the question at the time.

From the beginning, I immersed myself in the job and immensely enjoyed my work with students. In an environment that lacked friendliness, the students were my friends. In my first years in the position, I developed the courses necessary for endorsement in bilingual and ESL education. I also wrote training grants, which were funded. Besides teaching the bilingual/ESL courses, I was assigned to teach a social studies methods class in the undergraduate program and to supervise bilingual student teachers. How did I do all of this? When I think about it now, my only explanation is that I was young and full of energy. Also, I knew that if I did not teach the bilingual education courses, no one else would. My commitment to the goals of the program compelled me to agree to teach more courses than anyone else in the college was teaching. Needless to say, preparing for classes took a lot of my time.

Meanwhile, what was happening to my research and publication record? During my first NIE grant, I had collected data related to literacy in bilingual classrooms. Also, during the year I was away from the university, I received a second NIE grant to study the linguistic characteristics and discourse patterns in both Spanish and English of bilingual children at different levels of proficiency. Using these data sets, I wrote manuscripts and sent them to different journals for review. I published several papers in the few existing bilingual journals and several book chapters. Other papers were sent to mainstream journals whose reviewers were neither knowledgeable about nor interested in bilingualism or bilingual education. Their reviews were completely useless. Several papers were reviewed and turned down, even when it was obvious that the reviewers did not understand the purpose or even the content of the manuscripts. It was very disconcerting to know that, even when I received comments that could lead to resubmissions, the comments were useless. They were asking me to change the content of the paper or the conceptual framework of my research to fit paradigms that I was not pursuing or that were irrelevant to my research agenda.

Eventually, I gave up sending manuscripts to mainstream journals and published mainly in bilingual and second-language journals. The people who evaluated my work at the college did not view this situation favorably. They did not know the journals in which I published, and that diminished the value of my publications. I was always told that I might not get tenure unless I published in major educational journals. I was playing the game, but in an uneven manner. Through all of this, I never received any support from tenured faculty members with regard to my publication record.

I did become very successful in obtaining grants to support the teacher training program, however, and these grants made it possible to hire adjunct faculty to teach courses in the program. Over the years, the program has grown to include graduate students as well. We also have offered fellowships for students pursuing Ph.D.s; these students do their research on topics related to the educational needs of culturally and linguistically diverse children.

While playing the game, I have always followed my vision of the public good. I found myself at the margin of university activities, but in a space that fulfilled the civic mission of the university. I have been part of UIC for most of my academic life. Every time I have presented my record, first for tenure and promotion to associate professor and then for promotion to full professor, I have been advised that I might not make it. But when my record of research, teaching, and service is presented within the context of the program I coordinate, I have not been denied. I have made it in academia following an alternate route, my own vision, while also fulfilling the university's vision of the public good. This has not been overlooked. My work has become relevant to the college and the university mission because I have successfully recruited and retained undergraduate and graduate students. I also have been able to build a research and publication record that, although not comparable to other faculty members of the same rank, is recognized in the field.

My service agenda includes work in the schools and the community. Serving the needs of the community is an important part of the land-grant, urban university's mission. It is hard for faculty with only academic goals in mind to understand and participate in this work for the public good, but it always has been natural for me.

My service to the community now includes a commitment to train not only bilingual/ESL teachers, but *all* teachers, and I also work with families in the Latino community in Chicago. These two endeavors have allowed me to tie my research to my service initiatives. I am currently involved in a project with both bilingual and "regular" teachers in 15 schools in Chicago. These teachers are learning to collaborate in support of the needs of the second-language learners at their respective schools. Many of their schools are going through changes with plans developed by their own teachers; and they are achieving their goals.

For the last 16 years, I have been involved in a large community project in Chicago's Latino community. With a colleague, I developed a family literacy program, Project FLAME (Family Literacy: *Aprendiendo, Mejorando, Educando*) in 1989. While the original program design was based on what we thought would help new immigrant families in supporting their children's learning at home, over the years the parents have taken over the program. Its literacy components have been kept intact, but the delivery and program activities are carried out in ways that are more relevant to the parents. This has led to development of a theoretical framework and underlying principles for the program based on respect for the knowledge that parents bring to the learning situation and acceptance of cultural ways of learning and teaching that occur at home. We are helping parents expand their methods of enhancing literacy at home and creating a bridge between home and school. This bridge facilitates their children's transition between home and school. My work with parents in the Pilsen community in Chicago is the highlight of my life; I am learning so much from them.

Throughout my years in academia, participation in professional organizations has helped me to understand how to play the academia game. The American Educational Research Association (AERA) was particularly helpful. I first participated in an AERA annual meeting as a graduate student in 1973. Since then, I have yet to miss a meeting. In the '70s, NIE training at AERA taught me about academic and grant writing. I also was able to participate in a network of minority scholars who shared a similar vision of the common good. Many of these people were Latinos. Working together, we formed the Bilingual Education Special Interest Group (SIG) in 1975 and the Hispanic Research SIG two or three years later. These structures within AERA have allowed Latinos to share their research and to network and show support for one another across generations. The connections made at AERA have supported younger colleagues while they looked for academic positions and pursued their tenure and promotion endeavors. Through other professional organizations, I have learned how to become part of academic networks that support, review, and publish each others' work. Though I have not taken advantage of my acceptance into these groups to publish much of my work, I have been able to review manuscripts that deal with Latino students' education. My hope is that my reviews are fair and useful to authors as they publish or resubmit their papers for publication. I do not want anyone to have the experiences that I had many years ago when I submitted manuscripts to major mainstream journals.

I Have Done It My Way . . . So Far

How do I feel about my academic life? I have been able to construct my own (private) vision of the public good and work for it in a space that has grown to appreciate the group I represent: Latinos in the United States. Through it all, I have been able to use a vision of the world and a social conscience I learned from my family long ago. I developed an agenda that included research, teaching, and service to fit my vision of the public good and, to some degree, the university's agenda. I played the academic game on my own terms, with dignity and hard work. The Latino social consciousness (*conciencia social*) I learned at home has survived through the years, and it has helped me stay true to my values. My social consciousness and commitment to serve Latinos in the United States have allowed me to take chances, be proactive, and be passionate about my work.

More and more often, people ask me when I am going to retire. I guess I have been around for a long time. The more I think about it, the more I feel I should stay in academia for a few more years. I do love my job. I greatly enjoy working with students, many of them Latinos, at all education levels. I am learning so much as I work with teachers in schools and parents in the community. I am still collecting data while I work with teachers and parents. I have more time to write and, I hope, to publish more of my work.

At the university, the bilingual/ESL program is an integral part of our College of Education. Today, we have six faculty members in the program and several Latino colleagues on the faculty. One of my main concerns is new faculty being overly burdened with administrative or extra duties as they work toward tenure. I do not want anyone to have the experience I had when I was a newly hired professor.

Our program is respected, and we still have grants to support a large number of students. With all of this happening, why retire now? I still have a commitment to a vision of the public good that, in many ways, is more possible than ever before. I'll be around for a few more years.

When I reflect on my time in academia, some questions come to mind. Did I contribute to the public good? I feel I did. Was my vision of the public good the same as that of my institution's? Probably not, but some of my academic work has been recognized by professional organizations, students, and alumni.

After all these years, what would I change to allow diverse faculty to serve society better? I think that universities have to start valuing different types of scholarship and encourage faculty to develop academic agendas (or spaces) that connect service to research, and they should allow and encourage the coexistence of multiple views of the public good in their midst. Academia should learn to respect multiple research perspectives, academic interests, and voices.

Reference

Ellis, C., & Bochner, A. B. (2000). Autoethnography, personal narrative, reflexivity: Researcher as subject. In N. K. Denzin & Y. S. Lincoln (Eds.), *Handbook of qualitative research* (pp. 733–768). Thousand Oaks, CA: Sage.

9

IN SEARCH OF PRAXIS

Legacy Making in the Aggregate

Kenneth P. González

A s I was preparing my thoughts for this chapter, I learned that my father had died. My father was not supposed to die; I had just seen him three days earlier. I sat across from him as our family gathered at a local restaurant to celebrate my younger sister's birthday. I can still see him in my mind, sitting there across from me. We're talking about a recent soccer game between the United States and Mexico. Mexico won. I'm watching him as he plays with my son, teaching him how to give a "high five." These are supposed to be the best years of my life with my father, now my best friend. My father was happy and healthy with many more years ahead of him . . . years for me to hug him, years for him to play with my son and daughter, years for him to listen and offer advice, and more years to be that model of humanity I strive so hard to follow.

My father was a sensitive and enlightened man. He did not study on a university campus; but he used his intelligence and sense of social justice each day as an activist and educator. For years, he volunteered at some of the poorest, underperforming schools in the city of San Bernardino, California. He tutored, mentored, and coached hundreds, and maybe thousands, of children throughout his lifetime. During the funeral service, a school principal walked to the front of the church and spoke about the impact my father had on the children of her school: ". . . a man like no other, he gave hope to children who were on a path of hopelessness," she said. My father's greatest skill was helping others to see the strength of their own humanity. He was fully committed to improving the lives of others through the process of edu-

My father, Daniel V. González, in 1970 at a meeting for Mexican American
correctional officers in Chino, California

cation. For him, it was much more than preparing kids for good jobs; it was about helping them to become better human beings.

I am my father's son. I developed my vision of the public good from his words and his deeds. Like him, my vocation is to facilitate individual and community development. I also believe education is the means to achieve it. The struggle for me, as a recently tenured professor, is in identifying the best strategy to achieve such goals effectively. I must confess that I am unsettled and even irritated at the lack of national progress we, as professors, have made on the educational achievement of Latinos and other underrepresented students. Our university libraries are filled with scholarly books and journals on the study of education, yet both national and state trend data suggest that the gaps between the poor and the rich and Latinos and Whites have not improved significantly in the last three decades (Adelman, 2006). I sit here, troubled, with the thought that, upon my retirement as a professor in education, the gaps will remain.

I am not so naïve as to believe that one professor can turn the tide of Latinas/os' academic achievement. However, I believe it is essential to constantly reflect on how our efforts have contributed, or have not, to this effort. In this essay, I offer a self-assessment of how my work as a professor has contributed to the academic achievement of Latinas/os. I approached this writing exercise with the hope of illuminating what I did right and what I did wrong in my efforts to serve the public good. I took time to pause and consider what my father would do and what he would say. I hope the outcome of this work will enable me to be more intentional about what I do and how I do it. I begin with reflections on my first year as a tenure-track faculty member and conclude with considerations for my work in the future.

Part One: Panic and Doubt in the First Year

> Journal Entry, October 3, 1998: What am I doing here? This doesn't feel right to me. My first two months as a professor and I feel like an imposter. I have no idea what I'm teaching in one of my three classes, and I'm sensing that my students are starting to wonder about me. I feel strong in some areas and completely lost in others. I don't know who to turn to. I feel alone, alienated. I came to California with the expectation that there would be a critical mass of Latino professors. What I've found is that I'm one of four Latina/o professors in a college of education that houses more than 55

full-time faculty. I ask myself, "Why did I take this professor path in the first place?"

In all honesty, I did not enter a Ph.D. program with the intention of becoming a professor. As someone who worked in student services, I wanted to bring about change on a college campus in the role of an administrator. Since my days as an undergraduate, I sought to improve the access, retention, and graduation rates of Latinas/os in college. I had a strategy for social change going into my doctoral program, which was earning the necessary credentials to acquire a position of influence that would allow me to expand the opportunity structure for Latinos in college. I knew how to work at the local level, I knew how to manipulate the system, and I was prepared to do so.

My decision to seek and accept a faculty position was rooted in three areas: (1) it was what my advisor and many of my mentors wanted me to do, (2) I was sincerely interested in both research and theory, and (3) I wondered what difference I could make as a professor.

To be clear, I did not begin my work as a professor with a well-thought-out strategy for social change. It was assumed that simply becoming a professor was strategic enough. The dearth of Latina/o professors in higher education makes this point clearly. Latinas/os account for less than 3 percent of full-time faculty in four-year institutions, and even less among those who are tenured (Harvey & Anderson, 2005). But is the mere fact of being a tenured, Latino professor an indication of progress? I believe, for too many of us, the answer is yes. Perhaps a more productive question is this: How do we translate the existence of more tenured Latina/o professors into demonstrated, concrete changes for Latina/o and other underrepresented students?

Part Two: The Promise of Research

It took a good number of years for me to believe that producing empirical research could influence social change. This was a significant dilemma, given that the success of any university professor depends largely on his or her ability to produce new knowledge. I remember colorful discussions with my Latino doctoral student colleagues about the role and relevance of research. Some argued that research was a necessary evil: necessary because it was a key ingredient in obtaining tenure and thereby extending our opportunity to influence generations of students. It was thought of as evil because of its lack of apparent impact on real people's lives.

My argument for conducting research was twofold: (1) it allowed me to articulate a perspective that was largely absent, and (2) it allowed me to challenge existing, and in many cases harmful, notions of Latina/o student abilities and challenges. Where I believe I faltered was when I uncritically followed conventional notions of the purpose and sequence of research. From a conventional perspective, we conduct research to produce generalizable knowledge, naturalistic or otherwise. Sequentially, we begin by looking at national or state problems and the current knowledge base addressing such problems. It's all very formulaic: problem, literature review, purpose, methods, findings, implications. The limitations of conventional research are well documented—it produces narrow, fragmented knowledge, disconnected to the context of local environments (Lather, 2004).

I must say, however, that I do not fully discount the impact of my conventional scholarship. I believe it has opened up spaces for dialogue where there weren't any. It also has challenged existing notions of Latina/o students and provided new conceptions of how students succeed despite institutional and personal barriers. However, I am not satisfied with this level of impact. I am no longer willing to follow conventional methods of research. My strategy has changed. I seek not to produce generalizable knowledge, but rather local knowledge relevant to particular contexts. Problem identification no longer begins for me at the national or state level, but at the local level. This is the new direction of my research: producing local knowledge to solve local problems. The question no longer should be how my research will make a significant contribution to the literature, but rather how it will help solve local problems in a particular context. This is the approach my father would follow.

Part Three: Teaching to Transform

After a heated verbal exchange, a long pause captured the class's attention. The silence spoke volumes. A few students were looking around, but the vast majority sat still with their eyes fixed on one particular object. I could almost hear the voices in their heads, which were too complex to articulate at this moment. One student attempted; he raised his head and blurted out, "But . . . ," Without a helpful word to follow, he gazed back at the floor and continued to reflect. There were no easy answers, not for them or for me. "This is what teaching is all about," I thought to myself.

The antithesis of this experience is what we learn in workshops on the purpose and method of college teaching. The purpose, from an accreditation point of view, largely has to do with student learning outcomes and assessment. The logic is that, at the conclusion of any course, students need to have acquired specific knowledge, skills, or dispositions. Our task as professors is to teach and assess whether students have adequately achieved the specified knowledge, skills, or dispositions.

Similar to conventional notions of research, this perspective of teaching also is disconnected from local contexts. In terms of preparing professionals, there is the assumption of a generalizable knowledge base that students must acquire. Our work as teachers is to ensure that students have learned it. Unfortunately, little evidence exists that this approach to teaching professionals has produced positive outcomes for the students in our schools. K–12 settings remain replete with underperforming schools. Moreover, higher education institutions have not made significant improvements in retaining and graduating students, particularly Latinas/os and other students of color. How can we proclaim that our teaching is effective when our schools and colleges have not achieved any noticeable progress?

An alternative approach to teaching begins not with generalizable knowledge, but with local problems that need to be solved. Following this approach, students are immersed in a context of theory and action informed by local knowledge and guided by a methodology for social change. The outcome of our teaching centers not only on individual students, but also on the educational institutions with which they are working. Consequently, our success as teachers is determined by the extent to which our students have produced local knowledge and applied it to an institutional improvement process. I can think of no more important learning endeavor in the field of education than transforming an underperforming school into a high-performing educational environment for all students.

Part Four: Service: From Least to Most Important

Service has always been viewed as the least important duty of faculty work. During my first year as a faculty member, I actually received a list of the top

10 committee assignments that demanded the least amount of work. During a faculty meeting, a senior professor leaned over and whispered in my ear, "Pick the parking committee . . . it only meets twice a year." On most campuses, there are at least three areas of service a faculty member should fulfill: (1) service to the department, (2) service to the college, and (3) service to the university. In some cases, faculty members are expected to offer service to the community, which many of interpret as service to professional associations in their narrow field of study. Regardless of the number of areas of faculty service, the strategy is the same: participate in as few committees as possible. There is a strong rationale for such a strategy: far too many faculty members are denied tenure because of overextending themselves in their service efforts.

This is even more true for Latinas/os and other faculty of color. The dearth of faculty of color on most American universities creates a unique culture of obligation to both the institution and current and prospective students of color. Predominantly White institutions want to make sure that they have "minority representation" on as many committees as possible, which often means double-duty for faculty of color. Students, on the other hand, are desperately seeking role models or, at the very least, some familiar face to hear their concerns. The implication for faculty of color is less time for quality teaching and research (Viernes-Turner, 2002).

The strategy I followed during my first five years as a faculty member was to accept the advice of my senior colleagues and participate in as few committees as possible. Disengaging myself from mentoring and supporting Latinas/os and other students of color was not a strategy I considered. In every case, when a student asked for my help, I gave it. After a few years, I found myself chairing the dissertation research of every Latino doctoral student in the school of education.

After earning tenure, I engaged in a lot of reflection and soul-searching. The core question for me was, Do I want to live the next six years of faculty life in the same manner in which I lived the first six? The answer was easy: No. What took time was identifying an alternative strategy—one based on the community and not the individual, a strategy my father would follow. I found such a strategy in an alternative vision of faculty service.

Previously, my priorities as a faculty member were in the following order: scholarship, teaching, and service. The order of these priorities led to a disconnected and fragmented existence for me. With scholarship as my first priority, the questions that guided me were, How do I get published in a top-tier journal? And what will my specific, narrow area of expertise be? Replacing scholarship with service, on the other hand, produces not only a different set of guiding questions, but points me toward a new relationship of connectedness with my local community. No longer do I sit in my office writing about particular national problems. Instead, I meet, have lunch with, and discuss the needs of my community with local educators and community members. It is their needs that guide not only my scholarship, but my teaching as well. With service as my first priority, scholarship and teaching are used as viable tools to facilitate community development. My success as a faculty member no longer depends on the number of articles or books I publish, but rather on the extent to which my work has enhanced the development of my local community. This is the strategy I should have been following all along—a strategy with a greater promise to advance the public good.

Conclusion

My father used to always say, "Solve the problem and good things will happen." Somewhere along the way, I lost that message. It was drowned out by my own ambitions and by friends and mentors who wanted me to know what it took to be a successful faculty member. To many, I am a success story: a young, Latino professor who earned tenure early. Everyone, including me, was working under the assumption that producing a tenured Latino professor was definitely a contribution to the public good. But what problem did I solve? What can I point to that represents my contribution to the public good? In researcher terms . . . where's the evidence?

It is true that we, as professors, contribute to the public good in indirect and intangible ways. Through our teaching, we indirectly affect schoolchildren by preparing their teachers, counselors, and school administrators. Through our research, we use data effectively to inform and question institutional policies and practices. But the question still remains: "Where's the evidence that progress has been achieved?" It is the lack of such evidence, coupled with the words of my father, that compels me to change my strategy. It's time to solve problems, and not simply to end at understanding them.

References

Adelman, C. (2006). *The toolbox revisited: Paths to degree completion from high school through college.* Washington DC: U.S. Department of Education.

Harvey, W. B., & Anderson, E. L. (2005). *Minorities in higher education 2003–2004: Twenty-first annual status report.* Washington, DC: American Council on Education.

Lather, P. (2004). Scientific research in education: A critical perspective. *British Educational Research Journal, 30,* 759–772.

Viernes-Turner, C. S. (2002). *Diversifying the faculty: A guidebook for search committees.* Washington, DC: Association of American Colleges and Universities.

DOLORES DELGADO BERNAL

LA TRENZA DE IDENTIDADES

Weaving Together My Personal, Professional, and Communal Identities

Dolores Delgado Bernal

T he academy attempts to force us to teach and conduct research as if there is no meeting place among our personal, professional, and communal identities. The narrow expectations of many academic departments push faculty to divide, order, and disconnect these identities and place a priority on professional identity over personal or communal. Rather than detach and compartmentalize our identities, we might think of how the *trenza*[1] brings together strands of hair and weaves them in such a way that the strands come together to create something new, something that cannot exist without each of its parts. The *trenza* is something that is whole and complete, and yet, it is something that can only exist if the separate parts are woven together. Like the *trenza*, when we are able to weave together our personal, professional, and communal identities we are often stronger and more complete. At the same time, weaving together these and many other identities is fraught with complexity, tensions, and obstacles.

At every step along my academic journey, my professional, personal, and communal identities have come together. At times they clash, create much

---

[1] A number of Chicana scholars have used *trenza* (braid) as a metaphor to make theoretical connections to something that is encoded with cultural meaning. For example, Francisca González (1998) speaks of the *trenzas* of multiple identities and *trenzas* as an analytical tool that helps her to braid together multiple theoretical frames. Margaret Montoya (1994) speaks of conceptual *trenzas* as the rebraided ideas of our multicultural lives that provide opportunities for unmasking the subordinating effects of academic discourse.

dissonance, and cause emotional pain. At other times, they weave together in ways that bring a clearer sense of integrity to my research and a passion that motivates me to pursue academic work that can lead to social change. Anzaldúa (1987) and many other *feminista* scholars tell us that our lives, experiences, and identities cannot and should not be fragmented, and that it is essential to weave together our intellectual, political, and spiritual work (Ayala, this volume; Ayala, Herrera, Jimenez, & Lara, 2006; Burciaga & Tavares, 2006; Moraga, 2000).

In this chapter, I provide a *testimonio* that explores how I negotiate my personal, professional, and communal identities through what many Chicana scholars call a *mujerista* sensibility (see Delgado Bernal, Elenes, Godinez, & Villenas, 2006). A *mujerista* sensibility "takes a holistic approach to self that includes spirit and emotion, and recognizes our individual/communal struggles and efforts to name ourselves, record our history, and choose our own destiny" (Trinidad Galván, 2006, p. 172). For me, this translates into a way of life that requires me always to see myself in relation to family, community, the current sociopolitical realities, and a commitment to social change. A *mujerista* vision requires one to cross borders, learn from history, place a priority on collectivity, take care of oneself, and be committed to social transformation. A *mujerista* sensibility informs my reflections on experiences at different points in my life, the *testimonio* I wrote for this chapter, and how I attempt to live my life everyday. My *testimonio* "speak(s) not for the individual but for the experiences of a community—many Latinas in and out of the academy" (Latina Feminist Group, 2001, p. 20). While the details of my *testimonio* and specific context are unique, I realize that mine is a communal *testimonio*, not just an individual one. It's a communal *testimonio* because many other Latina faculty and students have had similar challenges, experiences, and triumphs. It's also a communal *testimonio* because most of what I research, study, and teach in academia is influenced, *con amor y con dolor*, by my communal experiences—what I have learned in my family and what I have seen in the communities of which I have been a part.

My Scholarly Beginnings: What I've Learned from *Cuentos*

> There is no definite, preset pattern for the way one will hear the stories of one's own family, but it is a very critical part of one's childhood, and the storytelling continues throughout one's life . . . So an individual's identity

will extend from the identity constructed around the family. (Marmon Silko, 1996, pp. 51–52)

I started working in Latina/o education in 1986 in a number of positions, ranging from a summer day-camp director to director of a bilingual pre-school, and from a parent involvement coordinator to a public elementary school teacher. Around this time, I also became very serious about recovering my family history and exploring the knowledge and wisdom that came from my family, what I later came to describe as my "pedagogies of the home" (Delgado Bernal, 2001). I collected old photographs, did census research related to my family's migration and settlement in the Midwest, and, most important, I interviewed elders in my family and listened to their *cuentos*. I've heard family *cuentos* all my life, especially from my father and two grand-mothers, who are all great storytellers.[2] However, as I was recovering my family history, I began to listen in a new way, and I was amazed by what I learned about my family and about myself. I listened with respect to learn and to understand, not to judge or disagree with what I was hearing. This is when I began to "put my faith in the stories, that language of the body, where the word is made flesh by the storyteller" (Moraga, 2000, p. 176). This faith in the *cuentos* allowed me to discover new ways of knowing, learning, and teaching and to embody the words of my elders.

Once, when my Grandma Eloise Delgado and I were looking at old photos, we came across a photograph of her and her sister on the farm where they did field work in Grand Island, Nebraska.[3] The photo took her back in time, and she told me a story that had taken place a few years before the picture was taken that demonstrates the creative ways she and other women enacted their agency and engaged in resistance within their domestic sphere.

---

[2] It's important to note that, although I don't remember my mom's stories in the same way, I learned and continue to learn from her more than from anyone else in my family. Her unconditional love, her dependability, and her unending support of me as a mother, scholar, and activist have been her teaching tools. I learned early on the strength and wisdom of brown women by growing up in the 1970s with a young Mexican American mother who went back to finish high school while I was in elementary school, and who always worked outside and inside the home. Clearly, my mom served as my first example of a *mujer* braiding multiple identities.

[3] Photos are snapshots of specific times, places, and moments, yet they do not represent an object of fact. In other words, their meaning and understanding is socially constructed. Even the most powerful images are only images without the context that's provided by a storyteller or narrator. According to Marmon Silko (1996, p. 20), a photo can add to the stories you've already heard and can elicit untold stories from those who are moved by its image. In my family I've used old photos in both of these ways: to elicit stories from my elders and to enhance the stories I've heard in the past.

She overheard my grandpa talking with his friend about a dance coming up on Friday night. Both men decided they wouldn't tell their wives so they could go to the dance without them. My grandpa didn't know that she had heard them talking. Thursday passes and Friday comes along and he lies to her and tells her he's "gonna play pool with the guys." She had just washed all of his clothes and ironed them with a flat iron, the kind you heat on the fire. After he told her he was going to go play pool, in her own words she said this:

> I went and got all his clean clothes . . . I threw them in the [wash] tub. I hurt myself [because I had to wash them twice], but he didn't go to the dance. He said, "Where's my clean clothes?" I says, "What do you mean, where's your clean clothes? They're in the tub." "Well, I seen them folded." I says, "Well, they weren't clean, I put them back, I'm gonna give them another scrubbin'." He didn't go.

My Grandma Delgado and Grandma Micaela Bernal's *cuentos* were powerful, not because they offered a "truth" of the past, but because they revealed to me how my elders made sense of the past and where we as a family have been and what we have experienced. They didn't explicitly tell their *cuentos* in terms of the intersection of race, class, and gender or even use words like "patriarchy" or "oppression." To them, their *cuentos* were the memories of the hardships, joys, and spirituality of everyday life. But by listening to the family *cuentos* in a new way, I could hear their strength, creativity, and resiliency. Through family *cuentos* and then *feminista* writings, I began to understand myself as a descendant of strong, resilient women and as a potential researcher and scholar.[4] Through my family *cuentos*, I also

---

[4] Chicana scholars helped me better understand the nuances and intricacies of resistance and resiliency by framing them around the lives of brown women. Hurtado (1996, p. 45) argues that to fully understand Chicanas' resistance it is necessary to understand the context of their oppression. She cites Emma Perez and Ana Castillo to illustrate how what might appear as "nonresistance" gains new meaning when understood within the context of one's oppression.

> She [my mother] feared my father's jealousy like abuse, and often stayed home to appease. I misunderstood her compliance. In time, I recognized her strength, his weakness.
> Emma Perez

> The sense of submission and docility that we see is . . . about survival . . . a powerful mechanism. It's like when you're in the ocean and a shark is coming; if you stay still, it'll go right by you. If you stay still long enough, and you survive it, then you can go on, and do what you have to do. But the nuances and the dynamics are intricate . . .
> Ana Castillo

came to learn how the history of my family and that of most working-class families of color had been silenced, creating a void in historical memory. These understandings led me to see how the *cuentos* of my family, the *cuentos* of communities of color, and the *cuentos* of women of color could all begin to fill a void in our collective memory and in the written history that is taught in schools.

Graduate School: Redefining a Space of Marginality

My family *cuentos* and my experiences with Latina/o youth as a community educator and elementary school teacher strongly influenced the trajectory of my research in graduate school. All of my professional experience was related to the education of Latinas/os and other students of color, and I knew my research needed to be connected to Latina/o schooling as well. It was my grandmothers' stories that moved me to recover a silenced history about Chicana/o schooling and women's participation in claiming educational spaces and rights. For my dissertation, I chose to study women's participation and leadership in the 1968 East Los Angeles Walkouts.[5] While this topic is very important to me, it was not necessarily so to the academic community in which I found myself. In an ironic way, my topic contributed to my sense of isolation and marginalization, as well as my sense of strength.[6] This auto-biographical reflection that I wrote while in graduate school relates my sense of isolation:

> Students who worked on projects with highly respected senior faculty were granted, by graduate students and other faculty, a higher level of legitimacy than [were] students working with junior faculty or on their own research. This reality was reinforced while attending a cohort meeting that was supposed to serve as a support group. I remember a [W]hite male student talk-

---

[5] Although the 1968 walkouts have been studied through a variety of analytical perspectives, none of these included a gender analysis prior to my research. Today the history and the role of women in the 1968 walkouts are more widely known than they were a decade ago. In March 2006, the HBO movie *Walkout* was released. It depicts the 1968 East Lost Angeles Walkouts from the viewpoint of a young high school girl, Paula Crisostomo. Paula is one of the women I interviewed and wrote about as part of my research on the school walkouts (Delgado Bernal, 1997, 1998).

[6] Much of this section is taken from the article, "An Honorable Sisterhood: Developing a Critical Ethic of Care in Higher Education," that I coauthored with three amazing women: Ramona Maile Cutri, Anne Powell, and Claudia Ramirez Wiedeman (1998). Our article examines how we, as four diverse women, developed a sisterhood based on a critical ethic of care that allowed us to redefine our marginal space in academia to a location where we gained intellectual and cultural strength.

ing about how he really was not respected in the program until he recently started working on a prestigious research project headed by an internationally known professor. He reflected on how this new appointment validated who he was as an up and coming academic. My turn followed. I explained that I did not work on a research project with a professor and that my research looked at an historical case of Chicana school resistance. Following his line of reasoning, I held no validity as a future academic. Not only did I not have the status that accompanied working on a well-respected research project, but I knew that my area of research held little status in their eyes. I never attended another cohort meeting.

Clearly, academic environments are laden with competitive hierarchies, rigid protocols of participation, and high-stakes consequences for how one demonstrates one's knowledge. What I didn't realize was the high-stakes consequences for *what* one chooses to study. It seemed that cultural beliefs and norms deemed certain topics of educational research "appropriate," and the value placed on working with high-status professors set a standard against which all graduate students were measured. Not measuring up relegated me to the margins and to a location where I was on the outside looking in, into a space where it was easy to doubt my intellectual abilities. I suffered from "imposter syndrome," not knowing when someone was going to find out that I really didn't belong in a doctoral program at UCLA. Despite getting good marks in all my classes, I continuously questioned and doubted my intellectual abilities because, after all, I didn't know who Foucault was, what the Frankfurt School referred to, or what "epistemology" really meant. Both the structural and cultural aspects of graduate school contributed to my sense of isolation—something quite common to women, students of color, and women of color in competitive academic institutions (Cuádraz & Pierce, 1994; Cutri, Delgado Bernal, Powell, & Ramirez Wiedman, 1998; Solorzano & Villalpando, 1998; Sotello Viernes Turner & Rann Thompson, 1993).

As I persevered through graduate school with strong support from two peer study groups and a faculty mentor, my situation changed somewhat.[7] My academic knowledge, skills, and confidence as a graduate student in-

---

[7] During graduate school I worked with a study group that consisted of the three women graduate students I name in the previous footnote, and I worked with a study group that consisted of three male graduate students: Juan Avalos, Mitch Chang, and Octavio Villalpando. These six friends offered me support and strength in numerous ways. In addition, Danny Solorzano, an assistant professor at the time, was (and continues to be) an incredible mentor and friend.

creased with time. Combining my sense of being an "outsider" with my growing confidence, skills, and different forms of knowledge allowed me to redefine that marginal space as a site of empowerment (hooks, 1984). My experiences in graduate school solidified the idea that I could not, nor did I want to, separate where I came from and who I was, from where I was going and what I wanted to accomplish in my life. While the second-class status of my chosen dissertation topic may have contributed to my isolation early on, my research topic also gave me a sense of purpose that was connected to what I was passionate about. In addition, I eventually found a wider academic community that valued and rewarded my scholarship.

My Brown Body: Embodying Multiple Identities

If the academy, in its very mission, denies the body, except as the object of theoretical disembodied discourse, . . . then what is the radically thinking "othered" body (the queer, the colored, the female) doing there? (Cherríe Moraga, 2000, p. 175)

Dolores Delgado Bernal with mentor Daniel Solorzano
at UCLA graduation ceremony

My body, my gender, and my sexuality are all parts of my identity and are with me in all aspects of my life. They have shaped, and been shaped by, the ways in which I participate in academia. Whether having to think about what to wear to limit how I might be objectified in a classroom setting, waddling across campus at eight-and-a-half months pregnant, having to be concerned about my safety after dealing with belligerent White male students who feel I'm a racist, or breastfeeding in faculty meetings, my brown body is always in the forefront. While I've had to negotiate patriarchal and sexist systems as a woman and a mother, as a heterosexual woman, I also realize that I have benefited in obvious and not so obvious ways from the heteronormativity of society. For instance, my current faculty position originally was created as a "spousal hire," something that is still somewhat uncommon in higher education, but almost unheard of for gay/lesbian academic couples. Not to acknowledge and recognize how my brown body constructs and is constructed by my academic world would leave out much of my story as a Chicana.

As a first-generation college student, I was the first of Grandma Micaela Bernal's 7 children and 18 grandchildren to graduate from high school and the first of Grandma Eloise Delgado's 6 children and 20 grandchildren to graduate from college. My family supported and celebrated these accomplishments with backyard graduation parties. I still remember the *conjunto* band my dad hired, and the visit from the police warning us to keep the noise level down. Yet, the idea of an 18-year-girl leaving home to go away to college on her own was so foreign to my family that they weren't sure what it was about or if it would work. I can still remember family members gathered in my mom's home predicting how long I would last in school. One family member said, "She'll be back next year pregnant." "No," said someone else, "I give her a couple of years before she's home pregnant." My body, my sexuality were discussed in front of me as if I were invisible. I didn't know how to respond, so I remained silent.

In 1999 my partner, Octavio Villalpando, and I started our first tenure-track faculty position. That same year, at the age of 35, more than 16 years after that high school graduation party and my family's predictions, I became pregnant with our first son. I gave birth to Olin in July 2000. Continuing in my tenure-track position, writing, teaching, and mentoring students, I gave birth two years later, in November 2002, to our second son, Izel. A year later, Octavio and I both put our files up early for tenure review. I remember a few *colegas* asking if I was nervous or anxious as my file was reviewed by the department, the chair, college, dean, and so on up the line. At the time, I was about six months pregnant with our third child, and we had a one-year-old and a three-year-old at home. I remember telling them that I honestly had no time to be nervous or anxious . . . at least not about tenure. I gave birth to our third son, Pixan, on April 23, 2004. Several days later, we received our formal letters announcing our tenure. While we were excited at the news and knew that it was an accomplishment and something to be proud of, we never gave our tenure a proper celebration. We did, however, give our son a warm welcoming with family and friends.

Clearly, Octavio and my sons put academic life into perspective for me and remind me daily that I have no choice but to weave together my mother, scholar, and activist identities. Maybe some academicians have a choice to do research that is interesting and important, yet disconnected from one's family, history, or experiences. Some educators are most comfortable with clear boundaries that compartmentalize the personal, professional, and communal. Recently, a local principal told me that she was both confused and frustrated by the fluidity of my roles as a parent, activist, and educational researcher. She didn't know which role I was performing when she interacted with me. She explained to me that she keeps her home role and professional role completely separate, and that she expects me to do the same. As a woman of color with a Ph.D. and as a mother of three brown sons in a working-class community, I would be irresponsible if I thought that these roles could be separated, especially in education. I can't be concerned with the educational outcomes of my sons only. While my sons are English dominant, have parents who understand the formal educational system, and have resources to support any educational need they may ever have, most of their friends have extremely supportive parents who don't have the same kind of resources, who are new to the schooling system, and who are not yet fluent in the language of the school. I can't stop my mother, researcher, and activist identities from coming together to advocate for the best possible education for my sons, their friends, and all of the children at their schools.

Spiritual Activism: Crossing Borders and Creating Possibilities

I constantly struggle with how to bring together my research and teaching in a meeting place that allows for the ways in which I embody being a mother, a scholar, and an activist. For more than two years I've been working on a community-based research partnership, *Adelante*: A College Awareness and Preparatory Program, with three close colleagues and friends.[8] Because most research on college student success suggests that the earlier students and their families consider college as an option, the more likely the students are to pursue higher education (Pascarella & Terenzini, 2005), we began a college awareness partnership with two kindergarten classrooms and their families at an elementary school with a Spanish dual-immersion program. While we continue to work with the kindergarteners from the first year of the partnership, every year we expand to incorporate the incoming kindergarten classes in the dual-language program. The school is 60% Latina/o, and more than 90% of the children are eligible for free or reduced lunch. Our vision of the partnership is pretty basic: We believe all young people in this largely Latina/o community should be prepared for, enroll in, and succeed in college, and we believe college preparation must emphasize students' intellectual development in relation to community and culture. To help create a college-going culture within the school, the partnership involves (1) regular visits to the university with hands-on academic activities for students and their parents, (2) university students-of-color mentors who volunteer in the classrooms weekly, (3) community *pláticas* where parents have a venue to voice their ideas and concerns, and (4) an emerging cultural enrichment component.

The three faculty involved in this partnership are also parents of children who attend this school, and the graduate research assistant volunteers as a university mentor.[9] We all live in the community, have a vested interest in the research, and are both participants and researchers. When the media, educational studies, or educators maintain low expectations for Latina/o children or refer to Latina/o parents and community members as lacking, uninvolved, unsupportive, or not future oriented, it is our brown bodies and the bodies of our children that provide the living connection between the deficit discourses and educational practices. Therefore, *Adelante* is much more than a research project or college awareness program. It is a school/

---

[8] For more information about the *Adelante* Partnership, see article and documentary: Alemán, Delgado Bernal, Villalpando, & Flores, 2006; Delgado Bernal, Alemán, & Flores, 2007.

[9] Enrique Alemán, Octavio Villalpando, and I co-founded this partnership. Enrique and I continue to co-direct and are co-principal investigators with the partnership. Judith Flores has served as graduate research assistant with the partnership for more than two years.

university/community partnership and "a way of life" to which we are deeply committed personally and professionally.[10]

My work with this partnership has become a kind of spiritual activism that allows me to cross borders between academia and community, to bridge academic work and what Jennifer Ayala (this volume, p. 25) calls "spirit work," and to weave together the personal, professional, and communal. It is not charity work, missionary work, or philanthropic work. It is not altruistic, because it is not selfless; I continue to gain more than I am able to give. It is not research that is objective, detached, or impersonal. It is community-based research that contributes to the civic mission of higher education and K–12 public education, but, more important, it is about transformation and breaking down barriers and recognizing the strengths within our community. It is activist scholarship that facilitates a type of border crossing for other Latina/o parents, most of whom are immigrants and have had little access to higher education. It is border crossing for young Latina/o students to see value in where they come from and who they can become. It is border crossing that encourages school staff and administrators to see those brown bodies that are often invisible to them and, one hopes, to engage the school community in a very different way. Finally, it is work that is difficult, exhausting, challenging . . . and work that feeds my soul.

A *Mujerista* Sensibility: Making Sense of My *Testimonio*

During the many months that I took to write this chapter, I was very uncomfortable writing in the first person. Clearly, a *testimonio* must be written in the first person, but the social scientist in me wanted to say, "Many Chicanas have experienced . . ." or "Most women of color in academia know . . ." instead of "I didn't realize . . .," "I came to understand . . .," and "I suffered from . . ." Only at the last stages of my writing did I realize that this discomfort was related, in part, to my uncertainty about the importance of telling my *testimonio* and my question about what lessons, if any, one could take from my *testimonio*. The answer to this question became much clearer to me when I participated recently on a National Association for Chicana and

---

[10] Francisco and Miguel Guajardo reminded us during the first year of the partnership that this kind of work is more than a project, program, or partnership. It is a way of life for many Chicanas/os in and out of academia.

Chicano Studies (NACCS) panel with Chicana scholars Larissa Mercado, Rebeca Burciaga, Julie Lopez Figueroa, and Tara Yosso. The panel, called *Cuidate Mujer: Chicana Resilient Resistance in Academia*, was designed for us to share our *testimonios* and theorize our experiences in academia. After our presentation to about 30 Chicanas and a few Chicanos, many *mujeres* became emotional as they thanked us for telling our stories and then explained how our *testimonios* helped them to interpret their experiences and simply know that they are not alone in their experiences. They were telling me, all of us on the panel, that it is important to share our *testimonio* because "the emotional force and intellectual depth of *testimonio* is a springboard for theorizing about *latinidades* in the academy, in our communities, and in our lives" (Latina Feminist Group, 2001, p. 2). I quickly realized the importance of my *testimonio* in this chapter and the power of telling others, especially other *mujeres*, about my experiences in academia. My *testimonio* will not remain a *papelito guardado*, but, rather, it is now written for other *mujeres* who I hope will write, share, and theorize their *testimonios* (Latina Feminist Group, 2001, p. 1).

After the panel presentation, we were also asked how we have the time to take care of ourselves and what we do to remain spiritually grounded. As I listened to the *consejos* offered by the panelists, I realized all of it, like my *testimonio* in this chapter, was informed by a *mujerista* sensibility—a Latina holistic approach to life that attempts to weave together intellectual, political, and spiritual work in the pursuit of community uplift. This sensibility reminds me that, to weave together a strong and beautiful *trenza de identidades*, I have to take care of my brown body before taking care of others in my work as a mother, scholar, and activist. This is because a *mujerista* sensibility is not based on selflessness, but on collectivity, wholeness, reciprocity, and transformation. Indeed, writer and scholar Norma Cantu reminded all of us at the NACCS panel of the sad reality that many Chicanas in academia now suffer from illnesses induced by stress and impossible workloads.

Clearly, a *mujerista* sensibility has also helped me learn from my grandmothers' *cuentos* and know the importance of understanding my family and community history. It was this sensibility that helped me redefine my graduate school experience and also better understand that process of redefinition today. My work on the *Adelante* partnership is spiritual activism with a *mujerista* sensibility that requires me to see myself in relation to family, community, the sociopolitical climate, and the possibilities of social change. A *mujerista* vision is what guides the braiding of my personal, professional, and communal identities. Like a *trenza*—these identities continue to overlap, merge, collide, and sustain each other so that the *greñas* become manageable. This chapter (and the NACCS panel) demonstrates the messiness of my *trenza* in the hopes that other *mujeres* will be inspired to figure out their own ways of wearing their *trenzas*.

References

Alemán, E., Jr., Delgado Bernal, D., Villalpando, O., & Flores, J. (2006). *Adelante: Una sociedad para el futuro*/Adelante: A partnership for the future. Salt Lake City: Utah State Department of Education.

Anzaldúa, G. (1987). *Borderlands/La Frontera: The new mestiza*. San Francisco: Aunt Lute Books.

Ayala, J., Herrera, P., Jiménez, L., & Lara, I. (2006). Fiera, guambra, y karichina! Transgressing the borders of community and academy. In D. Delgado Bernal, C. A. Elenes, F. E. Godinez, & S. Villenas (Eds.), *Chicana/Latina education in everyday life: Feminista perspectives on pedagogy and epistemology* (pp. 261–280). Albany, NY: State University of New York Press.

Burciaga, R., & Tavares, A. (2006). Our pedagogy of sisterhood: A testimonio. In *Chicana/Latina education in everyday life: Feminista perspectives on pedagogy and epistemology* (Eds.), D. Delgado Bernal, C. A. Elenes, F. E. Godinez & S. Villenas (pp. 133–142). Albany, NY: State University of New York Press.

Cuádraz, G. H., & Pierce, J. L. (1994). From scholarship girls to scholarship women: Surviving the contradictions of class and race in academe. *Explorations in Ethnic Studies, 17*(1), 21–44.

Cutri, R. M., Delgado Bernal, D., Powell, A., & Ramirez Wiedeman, C. (1998). An honorable sisterhood: Four diverse women identify a critical ethic of care in higher education. *Transformations, 9*(2), 101–117.

Delgado Bernal, D. (1997). *Chicana school resistance and grassroots leadership: Providing an alternative history of the 1968 East Los Angeles blowouts*. Doctoral dissertation, University of California, Los Angeles.

Delgado Bernal, D. (1998). Grassroots leadership reconceptualized: Chicana oral histories and the 1968 East Los Angeles school blowouts. *Frontiers: A Journal of Women Studies, 19*(2), 113–142.

Delgado Bernal, D. (2001). Learning and living pedagogies of the home: The mestiza consciousness of Chicana students. *International Journal of Qualitative Studies in Education, 14*(5), 623–639.

Delgado Bernal, D., Alemán, E., Jr., & Flores, J. (2007). Negotiating and contesting transgenerational Latina/o cultural citizenship: Kindergarteners, their parents, and university students in Utah. *Social Justice, 34*(4).

Delgado Bernal, D., Elenes, C. A., Godinez, F. E., & Villenas, S. (Eds.). (2006). *Chicana/Latina education in everyday life: Feminista perspectives on pedagogy and epistemology.* Albany, NY: State University of New York Press.

González, F. (1998). The formations of Mexicananess: Trenzas de identidades multiples. Growing up Mexicana: Braids of multiple identities. *International Journal of Qualitative Studies in Education, 11*(1), 81–102.

hooks, b. (1984). *Feminist theory: From margin to center.* Boston: South End Press.

Hurtado, A. (1996). *The color of privilege: Three blasphemies on race and feminism.* Ann Arbor: The University of Michigan Press.

Latina Feminist Group (2001). *Telling to live: Latina feminist testimonios.* Durham, NC: Duke University Press.

Marmon Silko, L. (1996). *Yellow woman and a beauty of the spirit: Essays on Native American life today.* New York: Touchstone.

Montoya, M. (1994). *Mascaras, trenzas, y grenas*: Un/masking the self while un/braiding Latina stories and legal discourse. *Chicano-Latino Law Review, 15*, 1–37.

Moraga, C. (2000). Loving in the war years: Lo que nunca pasó por sus labios (2nd ed.). Boston: South End Press.

Pascarella, E. T., & Terenzini, P. (2005). *How college affects students: A third decade of research* (Vol. 2). San Francisco: Jossey-Bass.

Solorzano, D. G., & Villalpando, O. (1998). Critical race theory: Marginality, and the experiences of students of color in higher education. In C. A. Torres & T. R. Mitchell (Eds.), *Sociology of education: Emerging perspectives* (pp. 211–224). Albany, NY: State University of New York Press.

Sotello Viernes Turner, C., & Rann Thompson, J. (1993). Socializing women doctoral students: Minority and majority experiences. *The Review of Higher Education, 16*(3), 355–370.

Trinidad Galván, R. (2006). *Campesina* epistemologies and pedagogies of the spirit: Examining women's sobrevivencia. In D. Delgado Bernal, C. A. Elenes, F. E. Godinez, & S. Villenas (Eds.), *Chicana/Latina education in everyday life: Feminista perspectives on pedagogy and epistemology* (pp. 161–180). Albany, NY: State University of New York Press.

LATINA/O *CUENTOS* SHAPE A NEW MODEL OF HIGHER EDUCATION FOR THE PUBLIC GOOD

Kenneth P. González and Raymond V. Padilla

O ur decision to use autoethnography (Ellis & Bochner, 2000) as a method of producing stories, or *cuentos*, was based on the assumption that linking personal experiences to cultural context would generate a deeper understanding of what it means to serve the public good. We were right in the narrow sense of that assumption. What we learned, however, was that the *cuentos* presented in this book offered much more. Beyond a deeper understanding of what it means to serve the public good, each *cuento* provided insights into *how* we, as Latina/o faculty members, came to understand the public good, developed an urgency to address it, overcame barriers as we pursued it, and reclaimed *estratejias* (strategies) to enhance it. In short, each *cuento* contributed to shaping a new model of higher education for the public good (see Figure 11.1).

Our model begins by uncovering the process by which we, as Latina/o professors, came to perceive and then know the public good. For the authors in this book, understanding the public good was born out of *cuentos* and experiences that occurred in a historical context of family and community. Padilla borrowed the concept of "organic knowledge" (González, 1995) to describe this process. He wrote, "knowledge acquired organically seeps into the very pores of our being, not just into our consciousness. It is not just a

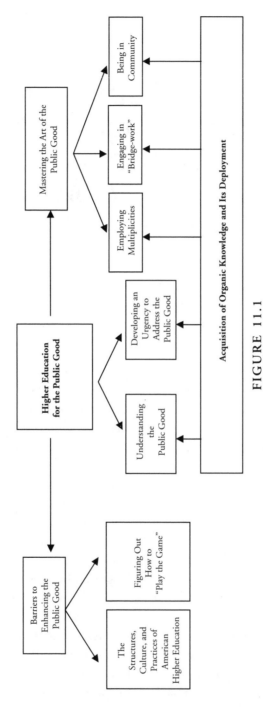

FIGURE 11.1

A *CUENTOS*-DERIVED MODEL OF HIGHER EDUCATION FOR THE PUBLIC GOOD

lesson to remember, it is a lesson to live by. This kind of knowing shapes how we think, but also who we are, how we live, and what we do with our lives" (this volume, p. 14). María Hurtado put it this way, "[these] experiences . . . launched me into a career that has made seeking the public good second nature to me" (this volume, p. 51).

The process of developing organic knowledge also created a sense of priority and urgency to serve the public good. For the professors in this study, serving the public good was not about serving a population or an individual that was unknown, foreign, or outside of our everyday lives. On the contrary, serving the public good involved an intimate and reciprocal relationship with individuals and communities that were viewed, in many ways, as family members. In fact, for some, the line between serving the public good and being in a situation dependent on the public good was quite thin. The Guajardo brothers made this point by quoting the following Mexican *dicho* (adage) shared in their family, "Yesterday it was me, today it's them, and tomorrow it will be my children . . . who need the help" (this volume, p. 69). This profound sense of interdependence was present in each story.

Despite gaining a deep understanding of the public good and the urgency to address it, each of us described a series of barriers that impeded and frustrated our efforts to enhance the public good. Overwhelmingly, the barriers had to do with the system, culture, and practices of American higher education. The educational system served as a barrier to enhancing the public good because of its historic legacy of racism and sexism. The vestiges of this legacy were experienced in the form of questioning the presence and quality of Latina/o faculty and the legitimacy and value of our scholarship.

The culture of American higher education also served as a barrier for the faculty in this book. Consistently, we described a university culture obsessed with image and reputation driven by a market mentality and measured by national rankings. Jennifer Ayala summarized this point: "In these popular college rankings, there is no serious measure of diversity and commitment to social justice work" (this volume, p. 34). As a consequence, the priority we gave to our vision of the public good was not viewed as a priority for the institutions in which we work.

In addition to the system and culture of American higher education, strongly ingrained institutional practices impeded our efforts to serve the public good. Many of us described a faculty rewards practice that did not take into account collaborative work with local communities. Henry Trueba, in offering advice to the Guajardo brothers, made this point, "Your [community] work is legitimate as a research enterprise, but you need to convince others in your academic departments that it is legitimate" (this volume, p. 76). His words clarify the reality that, in addition to putting forth energy to work collaboratively with our communities, we, unlike other faculty, need to exert additional energy to educate our colleagues about the value and legitimacy of this work.

At some point in our academic careers—usually early on—we learned that we were in an environment that held both promise and obstacles for us. The promise was the power of postsecondary education as a tool for individual and community liberation. The obstacles, like those described above, worked against our efforts and capacities to enhance our vision of the public good. Often, we were left with difficult decisions and lingering questions: To what extent did we sacrifice our work with the community to ensure that we met traditional standards and expectations? Conversely, to what extent did we ignore traditional standards and expectations in our call to enhance the public good? And, finally, what were the consequences to self and community as a result of the decisions we made? Luis Urrieta described the tension associated with these questions in the phrase, "selling out versus playing the game." "Selling out," as defined by Urrieta (this volume, p. 84), refers to seeking status and recognition exclusively for self-gain. Many of the institutions in which we work can be viewed as operating under this definition. "Playing the game," conversely, refers to strategizing our daily practice as Latina/o professors in a way that enhances the public good while, at the same time, being aware of the obstacles that accompany working in what Urrieta calls "whitestream institutions." Urrieta describes "whitestream institutions" as having "official and unofficial text . . . that are founded on the practice, principles, morals, values, and history of White supremacy" (this volume, p. 85).

Fortunately, the stories shared in this book did not end with a list of barriers impeding our efforts to promote the public good. On the contrary, each author presented his or her own strategies and approaches to enhancing the public good. It is interesting that many of us drew our strategies and approaches from the *cuentos* and experiences from our families and communities. In other words, the "organic knowledge" we accumulated from our homes and communities served as a source for not only understanding the public good, but also for creating and designing strategies and approaches to enhance it. The Guajardo brothers offered an example: "We learned at a young age that the *plática* was an act of sharing ideas, experiences and stories . . . It made sense that when we grew up and became teachers and researchers that we would use this same strategy. The *plática* as a method is authentic and . . . pushes the researchers' comfort zone, for without authenticity, the *plática* will not yield the necessary currency needed for building community and for conducting sound research" (this volume, p. 66–67).

In chapter three, Jennifer Ayala pointed out that we have the capacity to bring the strengths of our biculturality, code-switching skills, and other multiplicities acquired from our families and communities to the work we do as professors. She, like many of the faculty in this book, used such strengths to create bridges between local communities and the institution in which she works. She wrote, "this type of collaboration blurs the boundaries between community and academy, where the organization is enriching all of us . . . integrating our different selves, fulfilling a sense of wholeness and connection" (this volume, p. 35). This form of "bridge-work," as described by Ayala, was a common approach used by many of the authors of this text. For Dolores Delgado Bernal, it served not only as a strategy for social change, but also as a way to overcome institutional cultures and practices that "divide and disconnect . . . and place a priority on professional identity over the personal and communal" (this volume, p. 135). Bernal used the ideas rooted in the concept of *trenza* to overcome such fragmentation. She wrote, "rather than detach and compartmentalize our identities, we might think of how the *trenza* brings together strands of hair and weaves them in such a way that the strands come together to create something new . . . Like the *trenza*, when we are able to weave together our personal, professional, and communal identities we are often stronger and more complete" (this volume, **p. 000**).

Finally, the organic knowledge that we acquired from our families and communities also reminded us that our strength to endure and realize our visions of the public good depends on our ability to be in community with those around us. This was our most important lesson and strategy. Jennifer Ayala put it this way: "I am strongest when in community with others. Perhaps this is my/our work in the academy: the forging of healing connections among the community, academy, ourselves as an indivisible bodymind-spirit" (this volume, p. 34).

At the end of his chapter, Raymond V. Padilla argued that the key to enhancing the public good is to be art. In other words, we, as Latina/o professors, must be willing to "be active in real time, fashioning collective action into structures for the public good" (this volume, p. 23). The stories shared in this book provide examples of being art. Our model describes this process as using our multiplicities, engaging in bridge-work, and being in community with others. It is our hope that, as others consider and reflect on the *cuentos* in this book, they come away with a deeper understanding of the public good and a desire and strategy to master the art of enhancing it.

References

Ayala, J. (2007). *Voces* in dialogue: What is our work in the academy? In K. González, & R. V. Padilla (Eds.), *Doing the public good: Latina/os scholars engage civic participation* (pp. 25–37). Sterling, VA: Stylus.

Delgado Bernal, D. (2007). *La trenza de identidades*: Weaving together my personal, professional, and communal identities. In K. P. González & R. V. Padilla (Eds.), *Doing the public good: Latina/os scholars engage civic participation* (pp. 135–148). Sterling, VA: Stylus.

Ellis, C., & Bochner, A. B. (2000). Autoethnography, personal narrative, reflexivity: Researcher as subject. In N. K. Denzin & Y. S. Lincoln (Eds.), *Handbook of qualitative research* (pp. 733–768). Thousand Oaks, CA: Sage.

González, M. C. (1995). In search of the voice I always had. In R. V. Padilla & R. C. Chávez (Eds.), *The leaning ivory tower. Latino professors in American universities* (pp. 77–90). Albany, NY: State University of New York Press.

Guajardo, M., & Guajardo, F. (2007). Two brothers in higher education: Weaving a social fabric for service in academia. In K. P. González & R. V. Padilla (Eds.), *Doing the public good: Latina/os scholars engage civic participation* (pp. 61–81). Sterling, VA: Stylus.

Hurtado, A., Hurtado, M., & Hurtado, A. (2007). *Tres hermanas* (Three sisters): A model of relational achievement. In K. P. González & R. V. Padilla (Eds.), *Doing the public good: Latina/os scholars engage civic participation* (pp. 39–58). Sterling, VA: Stylus.

Padilla, R. V. (2007). *Res publica*: Chicano evolving poetics of the public good. In K. P. González & R. V. Padilla (Eds.), *Doing the public good: Latina/os scholars engage civic participation* (pp. 13–23). Sterling, VA: Stylus.

Urrieta, L., Jr. (2007). Agency and the game of change: Contradictions, *consciencia*, and self-reflection. In K. P. González & R. V. Padilla (Eds.), *Doing the public good: Latina/os scholars engage civic participation* (pp. 83–95). Sterling, VA: Stylus.

CONTRIBUTORS

Jennifer Ayala

Jennifer Ayala, an assistant professor of education at Saint Peter's College in Jersey City, New Jersey, is a U.S.-born Latina, the daughter of immigrants from Cuba and Ecuador. She earned her doctorate in social/personality psychology at the CUNY Graduate Center and is part of the CUNY PAR Collective. Her research has focused on Latina mother-daughter relationships, the experiences of students of color in college, and participatory action research with high school and college youth in urban settings. She is generally interested in college/community partnerships through research, traditional and alternative spaces of education for youth of color, and community health issues among Latinas.

Dolores Delgado Bernal

A former elementary school teacher and community educator from Kansas City, Dolores Delgado Bernal is the mother of three small boys, a community activist, and an associate professor at the University of Utah in the Department of Education, Culture, and Society and the Ethnic Studies Program. Her current research focuses on a school/university/community partnership designed to promote awareness about higher education and a college-going culture within a predominantly Latina/o elementary school. She is the author or coauthor of numerous chapters and articles, some of which appear in *Harvard Educational Review*, *Social Justice*, and *Frontiers: A Journal of Women Studies*. She is coeditor of the recently published *Chicana/Latina Education in Everyday Life: Feminista Perspectives on Pedagogy and Epistemology* (2006).

Kenneth P. González

Kenneth P. González is associate professor of education at the University of San Diego and faculty coordinator for the specialization in college counseling and student development. He also serves as an organizational development consultant for the national initiative *Achieving the Dream*, where he facilitates the planning of institutional reform efforts to improve the graduation rates for low-income and underrepresented college students. He recently founded the South Bay Collaborative for College Readiness, a nonprofit early college outreach center dedicated to increasing the number of students from low-income families attending college. His research appears in *The Journal of College Student Development, The International Journal of Qualitative Research in Education, The Journal of College Student Retention, Urban Education,* and *The Journal of Hispanic Higher Education,* and he is a member of the editorial boards of *The Journal of College Student Development* and *The Journal of Hispanic Higher Education.*

Francisco Guajardo

Francisco Guajardo, an assistant professor in the Department of Educational Leadership at the University of Texas Pan American (UTPA), taught for 12 years in a rural high school along the Texas-Mexican border and is a founder and director of a nonprofit Llano Grande Center for Research and Development, a group dedicated to developing public school teachers, administrators, and youth leaders. At UTPA he teaches courses on curriculum development, instructional leadership, and sociocultural contexts of education. He has published articles on the history of education, curriculum formation, and instructional leadership.

Miguel Guajardo

An assistant professor in the Education and Leadership Program at Texas State University–San Marcos, Miguel Guajardo conducts research into community building, leadership development, race and ethnicity, community as pedagogy, and university and community partnerships. He served as a Fellow with the Kellogg International Leadership Program and is a cofounder and chairman of the board of directors of the Llano Grande Center for Research and Development.

Aída Hurtado

Aída Hurtado, a professor of psychology at the University of California, Santa Cruz, is interested in the study of social identity (including ethnic identity), Latino educational issues, and feminist theory. Her publications include *The Color of Privilege: Three Blasphemies on Race and Feminism* (University of Michigan Press, 1996); *Voicing Feminisms: Young Chicanas Speak Out on Sexuality and Identity* (New York University Press, 2003; honorable mention for the 2003 Myers Outstanding Book Awards from The Gustavus Myers Center for the Study of Bigotry and Human Rights in North America); and *Chicana Feminisms: A Critical Reader* (coedited with Gabriela Arredondo, Norma Klahn, Olga Nájera-Ramírez, and Patricia Zavella, Duke University Press, 2003). Her latest book is *Chicana/o Identity in a Changing U.S. Society. ¿Quién soy? ¿Quiénes somos?* (coauthored with Patricia Gurin, University of Arizona Press, 2004).

Arcelia L. Hurtado

A 1993 graduate of the University of California at Berkeley and a 1997 graduate of Boalt Hall School of Law (UC Berkeley), Arcelia Hurtado has extensive experience as an advocate for poor people charged with crimes at both the trial and appellate levels. She is currently a deputy state public defender at the California Office of the State Public Defender (OSPD), where she represents indigent death row inmates in the California and U.S. supreme courts. Before going to the OSPD, Arcelia was a trial attorney with the San Francisco City and County Public Defender and the Santa Clara County Public Defender offices, where she litigated numerous jury trials at both the misdemeanor and felony levels as well as in adult and juvenile courts. Arcelia also sits on the Board of Directors of Women Defenders, an organization dedicated to providing professional, technical, and social support networks for female criminal defense practitioners.

María Hurtado

María A. Hurtado, who has worked in both the nonprofit and public sectors for more than 16 years, is currently director of parks, open space, and cultural services for Santa Cruz County. Before working Santa Cruz County, she was the acting assistant director and director of parks and community services for the City of Tracy. She also worked as the deputy director of parks, recreation, and neighborhood services for the City of San Jose and as assistant director for the Parks and Community Services Department of the City of

Watsonville, California. Before entering the public sector, she was executive director of Fenix Services, a nonprofit organization providing drug and alcohol counseling services, gang prevention programs, and a woman's residential treatment facility.

Raymond V. Padilla

Raymond V. Padilla, a professor in the Department of Educational Leadership and Policy Studies at the University of Texas at San Antonio, earned a bachelor's degree (Spanish language and literature) from the University of Michigan and graduate degrees (M.A. and Ph.D.) in higher education from the University of California at Berkeley. Professor Padilla is a former director of the Hispanic Research Center at Arizona State and a cofounder of the Department of Chicana and Chicano Studies, also at Arizona State University. Through his research and teaching, he has contributed to the fields of bilingual education, Chicana/o studies, higher education, and qualitative research methods. Professor Padilla developed the Student Success Model (SSM), which uses qualitative research methods to construct models of student success, in addition to HyperQual and SuperHyperQual software to manage and analyze qualitative data. The results of his research have been presented at major national and international conferences, and his publications have appeared in numerous books, journals, and electronic media. He also coauthored *Debatable Diversity: Critical Dialogues on Change in American Universities.*

Flora V. Rodriguez-Brown

A professor in curriculum and instruction, and in the Literacy, Language and Culture Program at the University of Illinois at Chicago, Flora V. Rodriguez-Brown received her Ph.D. in educational psychology from the University of Illinois at Urbana-Champaign. Since 1982, she has coordinated teacher training programs for teachers of second-language learners. Her research interests are in literacy and second-language learning, learning at home, sociocultural issues in literacy learning, and the home–school connection. Her articles have appeared in *The Reading Research Quarterly, The Reading Teacher and Education,* and *Urban Society,* among other publications.

Caroline Sotello Viernes Turner

Caroline Sotello Viernes Turner is a professor in the Division of Educational Leadership and Policy Studies and Lincoln Professor of Ethics and Education at Arizona State University. Her research and teaching interests include access, equity and leadership in higher education, faculty gender and racial/ethnic diversity, organizational change, and the use of qualitative methods for policy research. Her publications include *Diversifying the Faculty: A Guidebook for Search Committees* and the coauthored *Faculty of Color in Academe: Bittersweet Success.* She has served on the Board of Directors of the Association for the Study of Higher Education and on the editorial boards of the *Journal of Higher Education, The Review of Higher Education,* and the *Journal of Hispanic Higher Education.* She received her doctorate in administration and policy analysis from the Stanford University School of Education.

Luis Urrieta Jr.

Luis Urrieta Jr. is assistant professor of cultural studies and education and a Fellow in the Lee Hage Jamail Regents Chair in Education at the University of Texas at Austin. His research interests are in identity, agency, and social movements in education with a focus on Chicana/o and *Indígena* (*P'urhépecha*) education, citizenship, and social studies education.

INDEX*

academic
    barriers, for people of color, 107–109, 139–141
    barriers, to community service, 72–73
    corporatization, 32–34
    culture of measurement, 76–77
    culture shock, 48–49
Adelante: A College Awareness and Preparatory Program, 144–145, 144*n*
agency
    and activist scholarship, 145
    and personal responsibility, 70, 106
    playing the game and, 83–86, 90–94
    through research, 128–130
Alemán, Enrique, 144*n*
American Association for Higher Education (AAHE), 7
American Association of Hispanics in Higher Education (AAHHE), 7
American Educational Research Association (AERA), 7, 122
American G.I. Forum, 6, 7
"An Honorable Sisterhood: Developing a Critical Ethic of Care in Higher Education", 139*n*
Anzaldua, Gloria E., 31, 106–107, 136
Aronowitz, Stanley, 32
Association of Chicanos for College Admission (ACCA), 7
autoethnographies, about, 8, 87
Avalos, Juan, 140*n*
Ayala, Jennifer, 145, 151

Bennett, Stephen E., 1
biculturalism, 25–31

bien educado, 4–5
Bilingual Education Special Interest Group (SIG), 122
Bochner, Arthur P., 8
Bok, Derek, 2, 32
Boyte, Harry, 2
bridge work, 9
bridging
    academic and personal lives, 106
    creating communities through, 34
    multiple identities, 28–31
Burciaga, Rebeca, 146

campus
    commercialization, 2
    diversity, 106–109
Campus Compact, 2
cancion mestiza, 31, 35–36
Cantu, Norma, 146
Carmelo, 42
Castillo, Ana, 138*n*
Cervantes, Lorna Dee, 41
Chang, Mitch, 140*n*
Chicano Movement, 18, 22–23
    and commitment to public good, 5–8
Cisneros, Sandra, 42
civic
    mission of higher education, 1–2, 30–35, 84–85, 121, 145
    participation, student interest in, 1–2, 35–36
code-switching, 28, 31
Colegio Cesar Chavez, 7
Colegio de la Tierra, 7

*Italics indicates tables, bold indicates illustrations.

Colegio Jacinto Treviño, 7
collective responsibility, 70
colorblindness, 86, 90–92
commercialization on college campuses, 2
communities
    creating third-space, 34
    engaging students in work within, 33,
        78–79, 130–132
    finding, in academia, 48–49
community-institution disconnect, 64
community narrative, 63–64
community service, 1–2, 35–36
conciencia, 83–86, 91–94, 113
    social, 123
Coordinating Council on Higher Edu-
    cation, 7
corporatization, 32–34
Crisostomo, Paula, 139*n*
cuentos
    gaining identity through, 10, 136–139
    understanding community through,
        146
    understanding public good through,
        149–150
*Cuidate Mujer: Chicana Resilient Resis-
    tance in Academia*, 146
culture of measurement, 76–77
culture shock, academic, 48–49
Cutri, Ramona Maile, 139*n*

Denis, Claude, 85*n*
discrimination, 116–117
"Diverse Democracy Project", 2
*Diversifying the Faculty: A Guidebook for
    Search Committees*, 106
diversity on college campuses, 106–109
doubt, self, 31–32, 140

educational
    attainment, by race and ethnicity, *108*
    pathways, barriers along, 98, 100–104
Ellis, Carolyn, 8

faculty, women by race and ethnicity,
    109

Family Literacy: *Aprendiendo, Mejora-
    ndo, Educando* (FLAME), 122
Figueroa, Julie Lopez, 146
Flores, Judith, 144*n*
Freire, Paulo, 88–89

Gonzales, Rodolfo "Corky", 52
González, Cristina, 14
González, Francisca, 135*n*
Grande, Sandy, 85*n*
Guajardo, Francisco, 145*n*
Guajardo, Miguel, 145*n*

Haney, Craig, 56
Harris, Cheryl, 85–86, 92
Hispanic Research SIG, 122
Hispanic Scholarship Fund, 7
humanity, reciprocal context of, 67–69
Hurtado, Maria, 138*n*, 151

"I Am Joaquin", 52–54
identities, multiple, 10, 25–31, 58, 135–145
identity, development, 71–72, 136–139
imposter syndrome, 140
institution-community disconnect, 64
institutions
    changing from within, 83–85, 90–94
    creating non-traditional, 73–79
    higher education and diversity,
        106–109
    service as a priority to, 130–132
"Intergenerational Scholars Sympo-
    siums", 3

Jones, Delmos, 89

Kellogg Forum on Higher Education for
    the Public Good, 2–3
Kellogg, W. K. Foundation, 2
Kirp, David L., 32
knowledge, organic, 9, 14, 149, 151. *see
    also cuentos*

Latina/o, commitment to public good,
    3–8

League for United Latin American Citizens (LULAC), 6, 7
Lincoln-Juarez University, 7
Llano Grande Center for Research and Development, 64–65, 67, 73–79

making a difference. *see* agency
marginalization, 139–141
Martin-Baro, Ignacio, 28
mentors, 50–51, 55–56, 71–72, 74–75, 103–105
Mercado, Larissa, 146
Montoya, Margaret, 135*n*
El Movimiento , 18, 22–23
El Movimiento Estudiantil Chicano de Aztlan (MEChA), 7
mujerista sensibilities, 10, 135–136, 145–147
multiple identities, 10, 25–31, 58, 135–145

National Association for Chicana and Chicano Studies (NACCS), 145–146
National Hispanic University, 7
National Institute of Education (NIE), 118
No Child Left Behind, 77

Organista, Celia, 50

Padilla, Raymond V., 76, 149
people of color, 97*n*
    academic barriers for, 107–109, 139–141
Perez, Emma, 138*n*
El Plan de espiritual de Aztlan, 6
El Plan de Santa Barbara, 3, 6
pláticas, 9, 144
    forming reality through, 62–64
    teaching through, 65–67
playing the game
    and academic legitimacy, 140
    to affect social change, 90–94, 113

within whitestream institutions, 84–86, 120–121, 152
" 'Playing the Game' versus 'Selling Out': Chicanas' and Chicanos' Relationship to Whitestream Schools", 84, 91
Poder Latino, 50
Powell, Anne, 139*n*
private good vs. public good, 14–23
Project FLAME. *see* Family Literacy: *Aprendiendo, Mejorando, Educando* (FLAME)
public good
    culturally relative notions of, 85, 118–119, 149
    definition, 97*n*
    education as a, 98, 100–103, 103*n*
    as an extension of family and community experiences, 114–116
    vs. private gain, 14–23

Quiroga, Vasco de, 5

race, acknowledging in curricula, 90–91
Raza Association of Chicanos in Higher Education (RACHE), 7
Reidel, Michelle, 85
responsibility, collective, 70
Rodriguez, Julia Curry, 55

scholarship, activist, 145
scholarship, replacing with service, 130–132
self-doubt, 31–32, 140
selling out, 83–85, 93, 152
service as an institutional priority, 130–132
social change agents. *see* agency
social change, teaching through, 130–132
social conscience. *see conciencia*
social justice, 29, 33, 47–48, 113
Solorzano, Daniel, 140*n*, 141
spirit work, 30, 145

standardization, 32–34, 76–77
stories. *see pláticas*
storytelling. *see pláticas*

teaching for social change, 7
Texas Association of Chicanos in Higher
    Education (TACHE), 7
The American College President, 108
trenza de identidades, 10, 135–145, 146
Trueba, Henry, 75–76, 151
Trujillo, Larry, 55
Turner, Caroline S., 104*n*

Universidad de Campesinos Libres, 7
Urrieta, Luis, Jr., 85

values, cultural, 44–45, 46–47, 51, 57
    family experiences forming, 67–69,
    114–116, 125–127

transmitted through *pláticas* and
    cuentos, 62–64, 136–139
Villalpando, Octavio, 140*n*, 142, 144*n*
Villenas, Sofia, 87

Walkout, 139*n*
Watson, Lila, 35
White supremacy, 85–86
whitestream, 85–86, 85*n*, 91, 91–93, 152
Wiedeman, Claudia Ramirez, 139*n*
women in education, 107–109
Women's Crisis Support, 50
Wong, Dania Torres, 50
work
    bridge, 30–31, 35–36
    spirit, 30, 35–36, 145

Yosso, Tara, 146